English for Academic Research

Series editor
Adrian Wallwork
Pisa
Italy

This series aims to help non-native, English-speaking researchers communicate in English. The books in this series are designed like manuals or user guides to help readers find relevant information quickly, and assimilate it rapidly and effectively. The author has divided each book into short subsections of short paragraphs with many bullet points.

More information about this series at http://www.springer.com/series/13913

Adrian Wallwork

English for Academic Correspondence

Second Edition

 Springer

Adrian Wallwork
English for Academics
Pisa
Italy

English for Academic Research
ISBN 978-3-319-26433-2   ISBN 978-3-319-26435-6   (eBook)
DOI 10.1007/978-3-319-26435-6

Library of Congress Control Number: 2016932948

Springer Cham Heidelberg New York Dordrecht London

Springer International Publishing AG Switzerland is part of Springer Science+Business Media (www.springer.com)

Preface

Who is this book for?

This book is part of the *English for Research* series of guides for non-native English academics of all disciplines who work in an international field.

EAP trainers can use this book in conjunction with: *English for Academic Research: A Guide for Teachers.*

What does this book cover? How is it organized?

English for Academic Correspondence covers all the types of email you will need to write in your academic career: emails and letters, both formal and informal, to editors, colleagues, and professors. It also covers how to write and respond to a referee's report, along with some brief suggestions on how to write a research proposal and a research statement.

How are the chapters organized?

Each chapter has the following three-part format:

1) FACTOIDS / WHAT THE EXPERTS SAY

In most cases, this section is a brief introduction to the topic of the chapter. Occasionally, the factoids are simply interesting in themselves and have no particularly relevance to the chapter in question. However, they can be used by EAP teachers as warm-ups for their lessons. All the statistics and quotations are genuine, though in some cases I have been unable to verify the original source. The final two chapters do not have this section.

2) WHAT'S THE BUZZ?

This is designed to get you thinking about the topic, through a variety of useful but entertaining exercises. These exercises are designed to be done in class with an EAP (English for Academic Purposes) teacher/trainer, who will provide you with the keys to the exercises. The final part of each *What's the buzz?* section is a brief outline of the contents of the chapter.

3) The rest of each chapter is divided up into short subsections in answer to specific questions.

How should I read this book?

This book is designed to be like a manual or a user guide—you don't need to read it starting from page one. Like a manual it has lots of short subsections and is divided into short paragraphs with many bullet points. This is to help you find what you want quickly and also to assimilate the information as rapidly and as effectively as possible.

You can use the Table of Contents as a checklist of things to remember.

I am a trainer in EAP and EFL. Should I read this book?

If you are a teacher of English for Academic Purposes or English as a Foreign Language you will learn about all the typical problems that non-native researchers have in the world of academia. You will be able to give your students advice on writing effective emails and getting referees and editors to accept your students' papers. In addition, you will find opportunities for generating a lot of stimulating and fun discussions by using the factoids and quotations, along with the *What's the buzz?* exercises.

You can supplement your lessons with the three exercise books (writing, grammar, vocabulary) that are part of this *English for Academic Research* series, plus the teacher's book that contains notes on how to exploit all the books: *English for Academic Research: A Guide for Teachers.*

Are the emails and other examples in this book genuine? Are they in correct English?

All the emails are based on real emails. I have changed the names of the writers and their institutions, and in some cases I have changed the research topic that the writer refers to in his/her email or letter. The referees' reports and replies to these reports are also genuine - although in some cases you might find this difficult to believe!

Unless otherwise stated, all the examples are in correct English.

Differences from the first edition

There are three main differences from the first edition. Firstly, each chapter now begins with Factoids and a *What's the buzz?* section. Secondly, there are three new chapters (Chapters 7, 8 and 9) on writing cover letters, reference letters and research proposals. Thirdly, Parts 3, 4 and 5 of the original edition (on telephoning, understanding native speakers, and socializing) have been incorporated into a completely new book: *English for Interacting on Campus*. This means that this second edition is entirely focused on correspondence. Adding the new chapters and keeping the old parts would have led to a tome of over 400 pages!

Other books in this series

This book is a part of series of books to help non-native English-speaking researchers to communicate in English. The other titles are as follows:

English for Presentations at International Conferences

English for Writing Research Papers

English for Academic Research: A Guide for Teachers

English for Interacting on Campus

English for Academic Research: Grammar, Usage and Style

English for Academic Research: Grammar Exercises

English for Academic Research: Vocabulary Exercises

English for Academic Research: Writing Exercises

Contents

Chapter 1

Subject Lines

Factoids

- The first email was sent in 1971 by an engineer called Ray Tomlinson. He sent it to himself and it contained the memorable message: qwertyuiop. However, several other people are also claimed to have sent the first message.

- If every email that is sent in one day was printed, each on one sheet of A4, two and a half million trees would have to be cut down. If all the printed emails were piled up on top of each other, they would be more than three times the height of Everest and they would weigh more than the entire human population of Canada. If the printed sheets were laid out they would cover a surface area equivalent to two million football pitches. The cost of printing them would be equivalent to Spain's Gross Domestic Product for an entire year—around 1.4 billion dollars.

- Although the most common Internet activity is emailing, a "Digital Life" worldwide survey found that people actually spend more time on social media (4.6 hours per week, against 4.4 for email).

- The term *drailing* was coined in the mid-2000s and means emailing while drunk.

© Springer International Publishing Switzerland 2016
A. Wallwork, *English for Academic Correspondence*,
English for Academic Research, DOI 10.1007/978-3-319-26435-6_1

1.1   What's the buzz?

1) Look at your Inbox in your email account. Analyse 10-20 subject lines and decide some criteria for judging how effective the subject lines are. Compare your criteria with a colleague's.

2) Look in your Spam. Again, analyse some of the subject lines (without opening the mail itself!). What style do most of them have in common? How do you know that they are spam?

3) Finally, look at some of the subject lines that you have written. Do they match your criteria from Exercise 1? In some cases, might your recipient have thought that the email was spam?

****

It may seem unusual to have an entire chapter dedicated to subject lines, but more than 250 billion are written every day. Subject lines are crucial in motivating your recipient to open your email and to respond quickly, rather than setting it aside for future reading.

The subject line of an email is like the title of the paper. If readers do not find the title of a paper interesting, they are unlikely to read the rest of the paper. Likewise, if your subject line is not relevant in some way to the recipient, they may decide simply to delete your email.

British journalist Harold Evans once wrote that *writing good headlines is 50 per cent of text editors' skills*. The same could be said of the subject line of an email.

In this chapter you will learn how to write a subject line that will

- be easily recognizable and distinguishable from other emails in your recipient's inbox

- prompt your recipient to want to know more and thus to open your mail

- help establish a personal connection with your recipient

- summarize the content of the email so that your recipient will know what to expect even before reading the contents of the mail

1.2 Write the subject line imagining that you are the recipient

Think from the recipient's perspective. I lecture in scientific English, and I receive an incredible number of emails from students who use the words *English course* as their subject line. From their point of view, an English course is something very specific in their life—it is only 2 hours a week as opposed to their research and studies which probably take up over 40 hours. So for them, *English course* is very meaningful. But from my point of view, the reverse is true. English courses take up a big part of my week. So the subject line *English course* is not helpful for me at all. A more meaningful subject line would be *Civil Engineers English course* or *English course 10 October*.

So, as with the title of a paper, your subject line needs to be as specific as possible.

In many cases the recipient will be doing you a favor if he / she decides to open your email—your job as the sender is to make this favor worthwhile.

1.3 Combine your subject line with the preview pane

Most email systems display not only the subject line but also make the first few words visible too. It may be useful to use the first words as a means to encourage the recipient to open your email straight away, rather than delaying reading it or deleting it forever.

Using *Dear + title* (e.g., Dr, Professor) + *person's name* as your first words may help to distinguish your email from spam, as spammed mails do not usually incorporate people's titles.

If you adopt this tactic, then it is a good idea to keep your subject line as short as possible. If you can include any key words in the first few words, that too will have a positive influence on the recipient.

1.4   Use the subject line to give your complete message

Some people, me included, use the subject line to give our complete message. This saves the recipient from having to open the email. A typical message to my students might be: *Oct 10 lesson shifted to Oct 17. Usual time and place. EOM.*

EOM stands for *End of message* and signals to the recipient that the complete message is contained within the subject line and that they don't have to open the email. If you don't write EOM, recipients will not know whether they need or do not need to open the message.

1.5   Consider using a two-part subject line

Some people like to divide their subject line into two parts. The first part contains the context, the second part the details about this context. Here are some examples:

XTC Workshop: postponed till next year

EU project: first draft of review

1.6   Be specific, never vague

A vague subject title such as *Meeting time changed* is guaranteed to annoy most recipients. They want to know which meeting, and when the new time is. Both these details could easily be contained in the subject line.

Project C Kick Off meeting new time 10.30, Tuesday 5 September

This means that a week later when perhaps your recipients have forgotten the revised time of the meeting, they can simply scan their inbox, without actually having to open any mails.

1.7   Include pertinent details for the recipient

If your recipient knows someone who knows you, then it is not a bad idea to put the name of this common acquaintance in the subject line. This alerts the recipient that this is not a spam message. For example, let's imagine you met a certain Professor Huan at a conference. Huan recommended that you write to a colleague of his, Professor Wilkes, for a possible placement in Professor Wilkes' lab. Your subject line for your email to Professor Wilkes could be:

> Prof Huan. Request for internship by engineering PhD student from University of X

Sometimes it might be useful to include the place where you met the recipient. For example:

> XTC Conf. Beijing. Request to receive your paper entitled: *name of paper*

1.8   Examples of subject lines

Here are some more examples of subject lines. The words in italics are words that you would need to change.

Attaching a manuscript for the first time to a journal where you have never published before:

> Paper submission: *title of your paper*

Attaching revised manuscript to a journal where your paper has already been accepted subject to revisions:

> Manuscript No. *1245/14*: revised version

> *title of your paper*: revised version

Reply to referees' report:

> Manuscript No. *5648/AA*—Reply to referees

Request to receive a paper:

> Request to receive your paper entitled *title of paper*

Permission to quote from paper / research etc:

> Permission to quote your paper entitled *paper title*

Request for placement / internship:

> Request for *internship* by *engineering PhD student* from *University of X*

Chapter 2

Salutations

What the experts say

Within the academic world, and even in an informal society such as that in North America, addressing academics using titles such as Dr and Professor, may make the recipient more willing to help you. Using titles may also help to differentiate you from those students whose emails resemble text messages to friends rather than requests to top academics. You may also get a more successful outcome to an email request if you use some apologetic or slightly deferential language such as "Sorry to bother you but …", "I wonder if you could …", "I know you must be very busy but …".

David Morand, Professor of Management, School of Business Administration
Pennsylvania State University—Harrisburg

Indian English tends to be more formal than British and American English. In emails, Indians often use the word *Sir*, even informally, for example, *Hi Sir, how're you doing*. They also use phrases such as *Thanking you, Sincerely yours* and *Respectfully yours*, which are rarely used by British or American academics. Sometimes Indians mix English words with words from their own languages for example, *Yours shubhakankshi*. Young Indians now use phrases such as *C ya soon*; they also adopt SMS lingo: *tc* (take care), *u no* (you know), *4ever* (forever), *4u* (for you), etc.

Tarun Huria, Mechanical Engineer, Indian Railways

Chinese students tend to address their professors in this way: *Respectful Professor Chang*. The word *Respectful* or *Honorable* is the literal translation from a Chinese three-character word (尊敬的). *Dear* is not used as much in mainland Chinese culture as in English / American cultures because it involves intimacy, because to mainland Chinese people "dear" sounds like "darling," "sweetie," or "honey." In mainland China it is generally used between close female friends, girl to girl, and between lovers.

Ting Zheng, teacher

© Springer International Publishing Switzerland 2016
A. Wallwork, *English for Academic Correspondence*,
English for Academic Research, DOI 10.1007/978-3-319-26435-6_2

2.1   What's the buzz?

Make a list of typical salutations in your language that are used at the beginnings and endings of emails.

1) How many of these salutations have a literal translation into English?

2) Do you know the English equivalents for the ones that don't have a literal translation?

3) With regard to questions 1 and 2, do you know the formal and informal versions in English of the phrases you have written down?

4) Imagine you were going to write to a researcher called Saxon Baines, with whom you have had no previous contact. Which of the following beginnings would you use and why? a) *Dear Saxon* b) *Dear Baines* c) *Dear Doctor Baines* d) *Dear Mr Baines* e) *Dear Saxon Baines*

5) Now think about how you would address this researcher: Tao Pei Lin.

****

First impressions are very important. When you meet someone face to face for the first time, you probably take 30 seconds or less to form an impression of this person. Research has proved that it will be very difficult for you to change this initial impression. In an email you can form a bad impression within just one second. People's names are incredibly important to them. If you make a mistake in the spelling of someone's name (even by using the wrong accent on a letter), you risk instantly annoying them and they may be less willing to carry out whatever request you are asking them.

If you use standard phrases (see Chapter 14), rather than literal translations, you will ensure that your email looks professional. You will also minimize the number of mistakes you make in English.

In this chapter you will learn how to

- address someone—whether you know them, don't know them, or don't even know their name

- pay attention to titles (e.g. Mr, Dr, Professor)

- make it clear who your email is intended for

- use standard English phrases rather than translating directly from your own language

KEY 4) e, 5) Dear Tao Pei Lin

2.2 Spell the recipient's name correctly

Make sure your recipient's name is spelt correctly. Think how you feel when you see your own name is misspelled.

Some names include accents. Look at the other's person's signature and cut and paste it into the beginning of your email—that way you will not make any mistakes either in spelling or in use of accents (e.g., è, ö, ñ).

Although their name may contain an accent, they may have decided to abandon accents in emails—so check to see if they use an accent or not.

2.3 Use an appropriate initial salutation and be careful with titles

With Anglos it is generally safe to write any of the following:

Dear Professor Smith,

Your name was given to me by …

Dear Dr Smith:

I was wondering whether …

Dear John Smith

I am writing to ….

Dear John

How are things?

Note that you can follow the person's name by a comma (,), by a colon (:), or with no punctuation at all. Whatever system you adopt, the first word of the next line must begin with a capital letter (*Your …*, *How …*).

Dr is an accepted abbreviation for "doctor," that is, someone with a PhD, or a doctor of medicine. It is not used if you only have a normal degree.

The following salutations would generally be considered inappropriate:

Hi Professor Smith—The word *Hi* is very informal and is thus not usually used in association with words such as *Professor* and *Dr*, as these are formal means of address.

Dear Prof Smith—Always use the full form of Professor as the abbreviation Prof might be considered too informal or rude.

Dear Smith—Anglos rarely address each other in emails with just the surname.

If you have had no communication with the person before, then it is always best to use their title. Also, even if Professor Smith replies to your email and signs himself as *John*, it is still best to continue using *Professor Smith* until he says, for instance: *Please feel free to call me John.*

In many other countries people frequently use functional or academic titles instead of names, for example, Mr Engineer, Mrs Lawyer. However, many people in academia tend not to use such titles when writing to each other in English.

In the UK the most commonly used salutation, even in professional emails, is Hi. Although *Hi* used to be considered very informal, this role has now been taken by *Hey*.

2.4 Avoid problems when it is not clear if the recipient is male or female, or which is their surname

It may be difficult to establish someone's gender from their first name. In fact, what perhaps look like female names, may be male names, and vice versa. For example, the Italian names Andrea, Luca, and Nicola; the Russian names Ilya, Nikita, and Foma; and the Finnish names Esa, Pekka, Mika, and Jukka are all male names. The Japanese names Eriko, Yasuko, Aiko, Sachiko, Michiko, and Kanako may look like male names to Western eyes, but are in fact female. Likewise, Kenta, Kota, and Yuta are all male names in Japanese.

If your own name is ambiguous, it is a good idea in first mails to sign yourself in a way that is clear what sex you are, for example, Best regards, Andrea Cavalieri (Mr).

In addition, many English first names seem to have no clear indication of the sex, for example, Saxon, Adair, Chandler, and Chelsea. And some English names can be for both men and women, for example, Jo, Sam, Chris, and Hilary.

In some cases it may not be clear to you which is the person's first and last name, for example, Stewart James. In this particular case, it is useful to remember that Anglos put their given name first, so Stewart will be the first name. However, this is not true of all Europeans. Some Italians, for example, put their surname first (e.g., Ferrari Luigi) and others may have a surname that looks like a first name (e.g., Marco Martina). In the far east, it is usual to put the last name first, for example, Tao Pei Lin (Tao is the surname, Pei Lin is the first name).

The best solution is always to write both names, for example, Dear Stewart James, then there can be no mistake.

Similarly, avoid Mr, Mrs, Miss, and Ms—they are not frequently used in emails. By not using them you avoid choosing the wrong one.

So, if you are writing to non-academics, be careful how you use the following titles:

Mr—man (not known if married or not)

Ms—woman (not known if married or not)

Mrs—married woman

Miss—unmarried woman

If you receive an email from a Chinese person, you might be surprised to find that they have an English first name. Most young Chinese people have English nicknames, such as university students or even teachers, basically anyone who has to deal with foreign people. They are simply used for convenience (i.e., to help non-Chinese speakers) and they are also used in email addresses.

Thus, a good general rule when replying to someone for the first time is to

- address them using exactly the same name (both first and last name) that they use in their signature

- precede this name with an appropriate title

- adopt their style and tone. If you are making the first contact, then it is safer to be formal in order to be sure not to offend anyone. Then as the relationship develops, you can become less (or more) formal as appropriate. In any case, always take into account the reader's customs and culture, remembering that some cultures are much more formal than others.

2.5 Be as specific as possible when addressing an email to someone whose name you do not know

For important emails it is always best to find out the name of the person to address. This maximizes the chances of your email (i) reaching the right person, (ii) being opened, and (iii) being responded to.

However, on many occasions the exact name of the person is not important, for example, when you are asking for information about products or how to register for a conference. In such cases, the simplest solution is to have no salutation at all, or simply to use *Hi*. Some people like to use the expression *To whom it may concern*, but this expression is really no more useful than having no salutation.

Alternatively, you can write something more specific, such as

Dear Session Organizers

Dear Editorial Assistant

Dear Product Manager

2.6 If in doubt how to end your email, use *Best regards*

There are many ways of ending an email in English, but the simplest is *Best regards*. You can use this with practically anyone—whether you have met them before or not, whether they are a Nobel prize winner or a fellow PhD student.

If you want to be very formal, then you can write *Yours sincerely* or *Yours faithfully* - today there is no difference in usage between these two forms.

Best regards is often preceded with another standard phrase, for example, *Thank you in advance*, or *I look forward to hearing from you*. For more standard phrases, see Chapter 14.

Note the punctuation. Each sentence ends with a full stop, apart from the final salutation (*Best regards*) where you can put either a comma (,) or no punctuation.

... very helpful.	... very helpful.
I look forward to hearing from you.	Thanks in advance.
Best regards,	Best regards
Adrian Wallwork	Adrian Wallwork

2.7   Don't use a sequence of standard phrases in your final salutation

When writing emails in your own language, you may be accustomed to using a sequence of standard phrases at the end of your emails.

Imagine you need to ask your professor for a favor. When writing to North Americans, British people, Australians, etc., normally two phrases would be enough in your final salutation. For example:

> Thank you very much in advance.
>
> Best regards
>
> Syed Haque

The above ending is polite and quick to read. The following ending contains too many salutations and is also rather too formal.

> I would like to take this opportunity to express my sincere appreciation of any help you may be able to give me.
>
> I thank you in advance.
>
> I remain most respectfully yours,
>
> Your student, Syed Haque

Bear in mind that many people in academia receive up to 100 emails a day; thus, they do not have time to read such a long series of salutations.

2.8 Ensure your signature contains everything that your recipient may need to know

What you include in your signature has some effect on the recipient's perception of who you are and what you do. It is generally a good idea to include most or all of the following.

- Your name

- Your position

- Your department (both in English and your mother tongue) and university/ institute

- Your phone number

- The switchboard phone number of your department

- Links to your homepage, LinkedIn, Academia etc

Make sure your address is spelt correctly and that you have correctly translated the name of your department.

2.9 Avoid PSs and anything under your signature

When recipients see your salutation (e.g., *Best regards*) or name, it is a signal for them to stop reading. If you write a PS (i.e., a phrase that is detached from the main body of the mail and which appears under your name) or anything under your signature, there is a very good chance it will not be read.

Chapter 3

Structuring the Content of an Email

What the experts say

The longer the message, the greater the chance of misinterpretation.

Ricardo Semler, CEO, Semco SA

The fact that someone sends me a message does not automatically impose an obligation on my part to respond. So I've started to delete messages without reading them. … It's your job to make it interesting enough to get a response. You have to remember that you are not the only human being on earth writing e-mail messages.

Stewart Alsop, Alsop Louie Partners, columnist Fortune magazine

Executives at every level are prisoners of the notion that a simple style reflects a simple mind.

William Zinsser, communication trainer and Life magazine writer

The great enemy of clear language is insincerity. When there is a gap between one's real and one's declared aims, one turns instinctively to long words and exhausted idioms.

George Orwell, English writer

The easiest sentences are just eight words long. … By 32 words, you've lost them completely. … You'll lose more readers in the first 50 words than you will in the next 250.

John Fraser-Robinson, business consultant

© Springer International Publishing Switzerland 2016
A. Wallwork, *English for Academic Correspondence*,
English for Academic Research, DOI 10.1007/978-3-319-26435-6_3

3.1 What's the buzz?

1) On the basis of what the 'experts' say on the previous page, write five bullet points on how to write effective emails. You can combine info from more than one quotation into a single bullet point.

2) Do you follow a particular structure when writing an email? If so, what is it? If not, why not?

3) When you receive an email, how fast do you read it?

4) What part/s of the email do you focus on the most? Do you always read the entire email (including any text after the final salutation)?

****

Some working people spend up to 40% of their day emailing. Given that emails take up such a huge amount of our time, a clearly laid out email which gives the recipient information in its most accessible way is sure to be read more willingly than one long paragraph full of long sentences. Putting yourself in your recipient's shoes is key to getting your email read.

In this chapter you will learn how to

- write from the recipient's point of view

- plan your email

- organize the information in the clearest and most logical (and grammatical) order

- be concise and use short sentences

- avoid ambiguity

3.2   Plan your email and be sensitive to the recipient's point of view

Write what the reader wants to read, NOT what you want to write.

Think about the following.

- What is the goal of my email?

- Who is my recipient?

- What is their position in the academic hierarchy? How formal do I need to be?

- How busy will my recipient be? How can I get his / her attention?

- What does my recipient already know about the topic of my email?

- What is the minimum amount of information that my recipient needs in order to give me the response I want?

- Why should my recipient do what I want him / her to do?

- What is my recipient's response likely to be?

Write in a way that shows you understand the recipient's position and feelings. Even though you may be requesting something from them, you are at least doing so by trying to address their needs and interests as well.

Think about how your recipient will interpret your message—can the message be interpreted in more than one way, is there any chance it might irritate or offend the recipient, will they be 100% clear about what its purpose is?

Also, if possible try to think of a benefit for the recipient of fulfilling your request.

Remember that if you contact someone frequently, you cannot assume that they will know the reason for your message.

To learn how to write an email in which you criticize the work of the recipient see Chapter 10.

3.3   Begin with a greeting + recipient's name

If you begin an email simply with "hi" or "good morning" or with no greeting at all, it will not help the recipient know if the message really was intended for them. Given that your recipient will be able to see the beginning of your email without actually opening the email, if they do not see their name they may think either that the message is not for them or that it is spam, and thus they may delete it without reading it.

A greeting provides a friendly opening, in the same way as saying "hello" on the phone. A greeting only requires a couple of words, and on the recipient's part will take less than a second to read so you will not be wasting their time.

However, if you exchange messages regularly with someone and that person does not make use of greetings, then you can drop these greetings too.

3.4   Assume that no one will read more than the first sentence / paragraph

How much your recipient will read of your email depends on: if they know you, if they are interested in the topic described in the subject line, and how much time they have.

If someone opens your email, you can assume they will read the first couple of lines, but you cannot assume that they will continue reading.

So in your first two sentences it must be clear to the recipient that you are asking / telling them something important. If you make the assumption that people will only read the first sentence this will force you to construct an effective email.

3.5   Remind the recipient who you are when previous contact has only been brief

You can announce your name and where you met.

> My name is Heidi Muller and you may remember that I came up to you after your presentation yesterday. I asked you the question about X. Well, I was wondering …

Or without announcing your name you can simply jog their memory

> Thanks for the advice that you gave me at dinner last night. With regard to what you said about X, do you happen to have any papers on …

3.6 If there has been no previous contact, give reason for your email immediately

Begin by explaining your reason for writing. Avoid giving your name, which the recipient will have already seen before even opening your email. Here are two examples.

> I would like to have permission to quote part of the experimental from the following paper. I am planning to use the extract in my PhD thesis. I will of course acknowledge the journal, the author...

> I attended your presentation last week. Could you kindly give the link to the online version—thank you. By the way I really enjoyed your talk—it was very interesting and also very pertinent to my field of research which is ...

Note how the key information is given immediately. Even if the recipient reads nothing after the second line, it does not matter because all the key information is contained within the first line.

However, if the recipients read only the first two lines of the following two emails, the senders would not get the result desired:

> I attended your presentation last week. I really enjoyed your talk—it was very interesting and also very pertinent to my field of research, which is hydro-energy robotics, i.e. water-powered robots. What I found particularly relevant, and which I think our two lines of research have in common, is ... Anyway, the reason I am writing is to ask if you could kindly give me the link to the online version.

> My name is Ibrahim Ahmed Saleh and I am a second-year PhD student at the University of Phoenix. My current research activity can be divided into two broad areas. My first line research investigates a question of global governance...

3.7 Make it clear who should read your email and what it is you are requesting

The email below is written in good clear English. But it has a major problem.

Dear Sirs,

I am an enthusiastic and motivated 24 year-old Electronics Engineer with a special interest in RF. I have spent the last six months doing an internship at XTX Semiconductors Inc in Richmond. This internship was part of my Master's and regarded the characterization and modeling of a linear power amplifier for UMTS mobile handsets. While at XTX I studied linear power amplifier architectures and worked on RF measurements. I will be getting my Master's diploma in March next year. Thank you for your time and consideration.

Best regards

Kim Nyugen

Kim uses a concise style and gives clear details of his activities. But it is not clear

- who the email is addressed to

- what Kim wants

Does Kim want a job—if so, is he writing to the human resources manager? Is he applying to a summer school—if so, is he writing to the course organizer? The recipient has no idea.

When you write an email, you should always address it to someone in particular. Recipients feel much more motivated to reply if they have been addressed in person. It makes them feel personally responsible. If you simply write *Dear Sirs*, you are severely limiting your chances of a response.

Find out the exact name of the person to write to—from the website or by telephoning directly.

The reason for your email should be clearly stated as early as possible in the email. So Kim could have begun his email like this:

I am interested in applying for the post of junior scientist advertised on your website.

Or:

I would like to apply for a placement in your summer school.

Finally, don't assume that your email will be opened and read. Given that getting an internship is an important step in your career, it is worth following up your email with a phone call if you don't get a reply within 10 days or so.

3.8 Indicate to multiple recipients who actually needs to read the mail

If someone is on a mailing list, they may receive hundreds of emails that are not specifically for them. It is thus good practice to begin your email by saying who exactly the email is for and why they should read it, then those who may not be interested can stop reading.

3.9 Organize the information in the most logical order and only include what is necessary

The email below is to the session organizers of a congress. The sender is requesting a delay in the submission.

> Dear Session Organizers
>
> At the moment we are not able to submit the draft manuscript within the deadline of 10 October for the SAE Magnets Congress.
>
> The paper is the following:
>
> Manuscript #: 08SFL-00975
>
> Paper Title: Rejection System Auto-Control for a Hybrid BX Motor
>
> Authors: Kai Sim, Angel Sito, Freidrich Sommer – University of Rochdale; Gertrude Simrac, Kaiser Ko – Mangeti Industries S.p.a.
>
> We are very sorry but we underestimated the overall effort required to collect the results to include in the paper.
>
> We would be very grateful to you if we could obtain a delay of a couple of weeks for the draft submission.
>
> We are confident that we will be able to complete and submit the draft manuscript by 21 October.
>
> Best regards

Conference organizers receive hundreds of emails in the weeks up to the conference that they are organizing. Given that the success of the conference depends to a large extent on the numbers of people who attend and participate, the organizers are likely to read every email they receive. However, they clearly have to be very selective with regard to which manuscripts they accept. When writing to them (or journal editors) to ask for deadline extensions, tell them immediately exactly when you think you will be able to submit your manuscript.

It is also a good idea not to force the recipient to read a mass of non-essential information before you finally tell them your request. The above email could thus be rewritten as:

> I would like to request a delay in submission of manuscript #: 08SFL-00975 until 21 October. I hope this does not cause any inconvenience. Best regards.

You may think the above is rather direct, but the recipient will appreciate the fact that he / she only needs to spend three seconds on reading your email.

Here is another example of a short email which makes its point immediately and clearly.

> I inadvertently submitted my manuscript #08CV-0069 for the SAE Magnets Congress, as an "Oral only Presentation" instead of "Written and Oral Presentation." Please could you let me know how I can change the status of my paper. I apologize for any inconvenience this may cause.

3.10 Avoid templates for beginnings and endings

While preparing this book I analyzed a collection of around 1,000 emails that had been kindly supplied to me by PhD students, researchers, and professors. One thing I noticed was that the emails often began and / or ended in exactly the same way. This was irrespectively of the recipient and the reason for the email, as if the first lines and final salutations belonged to a template. The advantage of this method is that, provided the template is written in correct English, it is quick and easy for the writer.

The disadvantage is that the recipient may be forced to read information that has no relevance for them.

Here is an email from a student who has booked hotel accommodation for a congress.

> *I'm Carla Giorgi, a PhD student from the University of Pisa, Italy.*

> I'm the author of a paper at ISXC16.

> Yesterday, I booked my hotel room using the forms on ISXC16 website.

> I'm waiting for confirmation from you.

> Please could you tell me if there are some problems with my reservation, if it was not successful, and when I'll be contacted.

I apologize for my scholastic English, I hope to clearly have explained my problem.

Thanking you in advance, I look forward to hearing from you soon.

Best regards,

Carla Giorgi

What I noticed was that the parts shown in italics were a cut and paste from several other emails that Carla had sent (including a request for the source code of some software, a request for a copy of a paper, and a request to go to a summer school). The problem of doing this is that the recipient has to scan the mail to decide what is and is not relevant to them. It would have actually been quicker for Carla if she had begun from the third line of her email and ended at the fifth line.

Only write what the recipient needs to know. This will save time for both you and them.

3.11   Bear in mind that long emails will be scrolled

In long emails it is imperative to gain the recipient's interest quickly so that they will be encouraged to continue. Ensure that there is a topic sentence showing what the email is about, and what response or action you require from the recipient.

If you have written a long email, it is generally a good idea to have a bulleted summary at the beginning of the email, so that if your recipient is in a hurry he / she can quickly see the important points.

Everything you say must add value for the recipient so that they will read each detail rather than quickly scroll down to the end. However, you should also allow for the fact that they might scroll your email. Make it easy for them to do so by using

- bullets

- bold to highlight important words or requests

- white space to separate items

The email below is impossible to decipher because it is one long paragraph, the punctuation is poor and doesn't help the recipient, there is no white space, and the English is chaotic. It is also poorly organized and sounds like a stream of loosely connected thoughts.

Dear Kai

Yesterday, I talked to Hans and James who said maybe its ok to move the instrument for a few days but he didn't know the setting of the instrument etc that would be better to talk to other people first: Rikki and Kim. For Kim, its clear to her for us to measure using a different concentration I think she meant that "for measuring in interval of hours is possible so why we don't do this", but its clear now, that we need the first step to confirm the sensitivity of the polymer film, in any case, I can try to manage to put the film inside the multi-well and with longer cable so that sterile environment will preserved. In this way, it is possible as well moving the multi well box inside if the PQS measurement need (if the moving the PQS is so complicated). I'll keep you up to date. Regards.

When you have finished writing an email, show your recipient some respect by checking that it is comprehensible. Most people would get a headache trying to decipher the email above.

3.12   When you have something negative to say use the 'sandwich' technique'

The sandwich technique is a three-part email.

The initial part says something positive and tells the recipient immediately why they should read your email. If possible it should encapsulate the entire message, so that in theory readers could avoid having to read the rest of the email.

The middle part, which is the main part of the message, should be clear and concise and written in a neutral tone, even if you are in some way criticizing the recipient or presenting them with negative information (see Chapter 10).

The last part should reflect the initial part, i.e. say something positive.

So, the top and bottom of your sandwich contain positive phrases. The middle part contains the 'meat'.

To learn how to use this technique see 10.4 and 11.9.

3.13   Use link words in long emails to show connections and to draw attention to important points

If you have long explanations in your emails, you may find it helpful to use words that link your sentences together in order to show logical connections. See Chapter 15 for details.

3.14 Ensure that recipients in different time zones will interpret dates and times correctly

Researchers work in an international environment over many time zones. In the sentence below, it is not clear exactly when the server will and will not be available.

> For maintenance reasons, the server will be not available tomorrow for all the day.

The problem words are *tomorrow* and *for all the day.* As I write this section I am in Italy and it is 17.00 local time. In Australia it is already *tomorrow*. What does *day* mean? Is it my day in Italy or my colleague's day in Australia?

Thus, if your project involves researchers from different parts of the world, you need to be much more specific:

> The server will not be available from 09.00 (London time) until 18.00 on Saturday 17 October.

To avoid misunderstandings due to differences between the ways various people write dates, I suggest you always write dates as follows:

> 12 March 2024

So: number of the day, then month as a word, then the year. If you write 12.03.2024, then this could be interpreted as 3 December or 12 March. Some people also write: March 12, 2024, but I find this less clear as the two numbers are together and a comma is also required.

3.15 Be aware of the importance of an email—not just for you or your recipient, but also for a third party

It is crucial to judge the importance of an email when you write it. Some emails are considerably more important than others.

Avoid sending messages from mobile phones. They tend to be written outside of the office and generally in a hurry while in the middle of doing something else. I strongly suggest that if you have something important to say, wait till you are in front of your computer.

The email below is extremely important, not really for the sender himself or for the recipient, but for the student who is the subject of the email. However, the email was probably written in less than a minute and sent without being re-read or revised (there are many mistakes in the English and in the punctuation).

> Dear Professor Howard
>
> I'm Pierre Boulanger, and Iím a University of X professor. Our research interests include power electronics, energy conversion and electric motor drives design and diagnosis.
>
> I see on your web site that you research team is interested to receive foreign students. One of my best student, Celine Aguillon, is available to come in Boston to do research activity in the fields stated above. I will sent you a short biography and a C.V. of Celine. She will be happy to work in your laboratory and finally to prepare her PhD thesis.
>
> Im waiting for your reply.

Like the other example emails in this book, the email above is real: just the names have been changed and the name of the university has been replaced with X. Pierre received no reply. The thoughts of Professor Howard were probably:

- This person has spent 30 seconds writing this request, why should I spend my own valuable time in replying, or organizing anything for his student?

- The fact that the email is full of grammar and spelling mistakes tells me that Professor Boulanger is not interested in detail and he may show the same lack of interest in his research. OK, he is not a native speaker, but he could at least have used the spell checker.

- Finally, I am not at all clear about the benefits of having Celine in my lab. What exactly will she be able to help my team with? I get the impression that the benefit is really for Celine and not for me.

The result was that Celine missed a wonderful opportunity to work with a top professor at a top university in Boston. And just because her professor could not take the time to write a decent email. Obviously, there may have been other reasons why Professor Howard did not reply, but the more effort you put in to writing an important email the more likely you are to get the outcome desired.

Give yourself plenty of time to write an important email. Do a draft version and then leave it for a couple of hours. Then delete anything not absolutely essential. Leave it again just in case you remember any other info that you need to add or to ask for.

3.16   The last words

Many readers will only read your first sentence.

Those readers that read the whole message will often remember most what they read last. So ensure that your email ends positively.

Here are some sentences that give a positive feeling at the end of an email where you have used the middle part of the mail to say something negative (see Chapter 10 on how to make constructive criticisms).

> It will be great to see you at the conference.

> Thank you so much for all your help with this.

> I really appreciate your time.

3.17   Don't cc people unless strictly necessary

Don't put people in cc simply as an indirect attempt at sharing responsibility or to cover yourself against accusations of poor communication.

3.18 Be explicit in your the main text of your email that you have attached a document

Recipients often don't check that there is an attachment, unless you specifically use the words *attach, attached, attaching* or *attachment* in the main text. Ensure that you use a phrase such as:

Please find attached ...

Attached is ...

I am attaching ...

You will notice in the attachment that ...

Note that the phrase *In attachment please find* is <u>not</u> correct English.

Chapter 4

Building a Relationship and Deciding the Level of Formality

Factoids

It is possible to guess the gender of someone just be reading their email and seeing how they communicate in chat rooms. Research suggests that:

Men: supply answers, and tend to shut down dialog.

Women: ask questions, make offers and suggestions

Men: make strong assertions, disagree, use profanity, insults and sarcasm

Women: diplomatic assertions, polite expressions

Men: on chatlines - less likely to confess to not knowing the answer

Women: on chatlines - share more information, admit to not knowing something

© Springer International Publishing Switzerland 2016
A. Wallwork, *English for Academic Correspondence*,
English for Academic Research, DOI 10.1007/978-3-319-26435-6_4

4.1 What's the buzz?

1) Below are six extracts from emails. In each case decide i) what level of formality the email is written in (note there may be a mixture of levels, e.g. informal main text, formal salutations), ii) whether it is appropriate or not. If it is not appropriate, consider how you would rewrite the inappropriate parts. Note that the English grammar and vocabulary in the emails is acceptable; however can you find the recurrent mistake in Email 6?

EMAIL 1

Thank you so much for offering me a place in your prestigious graduate program.

However, I regret to inform you that I am unable go because I failed to gather enough financial support.

I really appreciate the time that you have invested in processing my application.

Thanks again for your help.

Sincerely yours,

EMAIL 2

Dear Madam or Sir,

I'm really interested in the Master's program in Innovation Management, but my undergraduate major is Advertising (Faculty of Journalism and Communications) and I took the GRE rather than GMAT.

EMAIL 3

Dear Prof Smartars,

I am interested in applying for the PhD project "Do PhD programs represent a good return on public money investments?". Before starting the application process I thought it would be wise to send you my CV so that you can tell me if my profile corresponds to the type of candidate that you are looking for. If so, I would also like to have the opportunity to speak to you about the project so that I have a better understanding of it.

EMAIL 4

Thank you for your interest in my profile. I do want to get a fellowship, as I believe it's always a good point on my resume. At the same time, I would like to start working on my PostDoc project as soon as possible. Would it be possible for you to fund me for the initial period, i.e. until I get a fellowship? I know this is common practice in the US and I guess it should not be a big problem for me to get one, especially if I become part of your amazing group. Thank you very much indeed and have a nice day.

EMAIL 5

Dear Prof. Brogdon,

Thank you very much indeed for your offer.

I'll be in Portugal starting September 1st, and I could come to Germany pretty much right afterwards. As Bochum and Munster are very close (I guess 30 min by train?), I thought I could also come to your lab to have an idea of the different projects that you guys are working on if you don't mind.

Thank you very much in advance,

Best regards,

EMAIL 6

Dear prof.

I am the Student of the Yamani School of Advanced Studies who is currently working with Professor Yamashta (Anthocyanins Project) at the Department of Biology.

As you probably remember, I asked You to have the opportunity of doing an internship at Your laboratory in Paris. What I would like to know is if I can still come to Your lab, preferably from May to July

Waiting for Your reply.

Thank You in advance.

2) Convert these informal phrases into formal phrases

1. Re your email dated ...

2. This is just to let you know that ...

3. Attached is ...

4. I'll call you next week to tell you what time I'll be arriving.

5. Thanks in advance.

6. Sorry that I haven't got back to you sooner.

****

In this chapter you will learn:

- some key differences between formal and informal English in emails

- that establishing a good relationship can lead to useful meetings and collaborations

- that although English uses *you* in both formal and informal relationships, it adopts other devices to show respect toward the recipient of an email

- how to adopt an appropriate level of formality when dealing with people of different cultures

4.2   How to judge the level of formality

Below are some guidelines to enable you to distinguish between formal and informal expressions in emails (see also 2.3).

FORMAL: LONG AND COMPLEX SENTENCES

If a phrase is long and / or complex, this is generally a sign of greater formality.

FORMAL	LESS FORMAL
We *have pleasure in confirming* the acceptance of your abstract for ...	*This is to confirm* that your abstract has been accepted for ...
Should you need any clarifications, please do not hesitate to contact us.	*If you* have any questions, please let us know.
You are requested to acknowledge this email.	*Please* acknowledge this email.
It is necessary that I have the report by Tuesday.	*Please* could I have the report by Tuesday.

It is important to be aware, however, that some short sentences (e.g., the first example sentence below) are not always the most informal and can also come across as rather cold. Writing in a telegraphic style can obscure the meaning from your reader, so always try to write complete and comprehensible sentences.

The examples below show how a simple concept, such as acknowledging receipt of a mail, can be expressed in many different ways from completely detached to quite warm.

I confirm receipt of your fax.

This is just to confirm that I received your fax.

Just to let you know that your fax got through.

Thanks for your fax.

FORMAL: MODAL VERBS

The four modal auxiliaries *may, can, could,* and *would* are often used to make a request sound more courteous and less direct. Compare the following pairs of sentences:

May I remind you that we are still awaiting your report on manuscript No. 1342/2 ...

We are still awaiting your report on manuscript No. 1342/2 ...

Can you kindly check with her that this is OK.

Check that this is OK.

Could you please keep me informed of any changes you plan to make to the presentation.

Keep me informed of any changes you plan to make to the presentation.

Would you like me to Skype you?

Do you want me to Skype you?

In a similar way, *won't be able to* is often preferred to *cannot,* and *would like* or *wish* to *want.* Both *cannot* and *want* tend to sound too abrupt.

I'm sorry but I *won't be able to* give you any feedback on your manuscript until next week.

We regret to inform you that we *will not be able to* offer your students any special rate for attending the congress.

The modal verb *may* is extremely useful whenever you want to give your mail a formal tone:

I would be grateful for any further information you *may* be able to give me about ...

You *may* also check the status of your manuscript by logging into your account at http://manuscript.zzxx.com/account.

To whom it *may* concern.

May I thank you for your help in this matter.

Note: The use of *shall* as a future auxiliary and *should* as a conditional auxiliary is outdated in English, and their use is a sure sign of formality. In the examples below, the first sentence in each pair is very formal, and the second sentence is normal English.

We *shall* give your request our prompt attention.

= We *will* deal with your request as soon as possible.

I *should be glad if you could* send the file again, this time as a pdf.

= *Please could you* send the file again, this time as a pdf.

FORMAL: NOUNS

The English language is essentially verb based. Many other languages are noun based. When there is a predominance of nouns rather than verbs, it gives an email a feeling of distance and formality:

Please inform me of the time of your *arrival*.

Please let me know when you *will be arriving*.

To the best of our *knowledge*.

As far as we *know*.

For more on this topic, see 5.4 in the companion volume *English for Writing Research Papers*.

FORMAL: MULTI-SYLLABLE WORDS

Generally, a clear indication of formality is given by the number of syllables in a word—the more there are, the more formal the email is likely to be. If you speak French, Italian, Portuguese, Romanian, or Spanish, a good tip is if the multi-syllable word in English looks similar to a word that you have in your own language, then it is probably formal in English. Compare the following pairs of verbs. The first verb is multi-syllable and formal, and the second is monosyllable or a phrasal verb:

advise / let someone know, apologize / be sorry, assist / help, attempt / try, clarify / make clear, commence / start, consider / think about, contact / get in touch, enter / go in, evaluate / look into, examine / look at, inform / tell, perform / carry out, receive / get, reply / get back to, require / want, utilize / use

The same also applies to nouns, for example, *possibility* vs *chance*.

OMISSION OF SUBJECT AND OTHER PARTS OF SPEECH

A clear sign that an email is informal is when the subject of the verb and / or the auxiliary are missing. An email is even more informal when articles, possessive adjectives, etc. are also missed out in telegraphic style (last example).

INFORMAL	FORMAL
Been very busy recently.	*I have been* very busy recently.
Appreciate your early reply.	*I would appreciate* your early reply.
Hope to hear from you soon.	*I hope* to hear from you soon.
Speak to you soon.	*I will speak* to you soon.
Looking forward to your reply.	*I am looking* forward to your reply.
Will be in touch.	*I will* be in touch.
Just a quick update on …	*This is just* a quick update on …
Have forwarded Carlos *copy* of *ppt* to *personal* email too.	I have forwarded Carlos *a copy* of *the presentation* to *his personal* email too.

ABBREVIATIONS AND ACRONYMS

Some abbreviations are perfectly acceptable even in a formal email, such as *re* (regarding) and *C/A* (bank current account). Others, however, such as *ack* (acknowledge, acknowledgement), *tx* (thanks), and *rgds* (regards), should be used with caution—they give the impression that you could not find the time to write the words out in full.

SMILEYS

A smiley is a clear indication of informality. I strongly suggest that you use them only if your recipient has used them first. There are some people, particularly of older generations, who find smileys annoying. Also, avoid using them with anyone when you want to make a difficult request seem lighter. For example:

Please could you send me the revision tomorrow :)

The above request for someone to revise a long document within a very short time-frame is not helped by having a smiley, which may actually make the recipient angry as he / she will certainly not be happy to do such a long task in such a short time.

4.3 Use appropriate language and don't mix levels of formality

Below is an email written by a PhD student to a professor. Much of the email is formal, as is appropriate given the student / professor relationship. However, the parts in italics are very informal, and are thus inappropriate.

Dear Professor Anastasijevic,

I hope you *have been having a really good time* since our meeting in Belgrade. I have started to prepare for my period in your *lab* and first of all I'm trying to get a visa*!*

I would be very grateful if you could kindly tell me how to obtain the DS2019 document in order to request the visa.

I would like to thank you in advance and *have a great Xmas.*

Cheers,

Lamia Abouchabkis

The following email from one of my PhD students sounds very strange with its incredible mixture of polite English mixed with chatroom / text message style.

Dear Professor Adrian

I am pleased that you enjoyed my presentation. Dunno how useful it is.

I am happy if u r ok wid it.

Best regards

It is always worth remembering who you are writing to, and that not all people of every generation write in the same way.

4.4 Note any differences in style and level of formality between English and your language

The English language has increasingly become more and more informal. Below are three examples of salutations from letters written by Benjamin Franklin, one of the founding fathers of the USA, in the late eighteenth century.

Your faithful and affectionate Servant,

I am, my dear friend, Your's affectionately,

My best wishes attend you, being, with sincere esteem, Sir, Your most obedient and very humble servant,

Such phrases today would sound ridiculous in an email, even in a very formal letter. However, similar phrases exist in many languages of today. For example, a French person in a formal email might say *Would you accept, sir, the expression of my distinguished salutation* (10 words), or an Italian might say *In expectation of your courteous reply, it is my pleasure to send you my most cordial greetings* (17 words). Such phrases in English sound extremely pompous and would probably be rendered as *I look forward to hearing from you* (7 words) or simply *Best regards* (2 words).

In fact, most languages in their written form tend to be more formal than written English. This formality shows itself not just in the choice of words and expressions but also in the length of sentences and paragraphs. Below is an email to a professor from a Bangladeshi who wishes to become a research student. The parts in italics would be considered much too formal by most Anglos.

Dear Professor *Dr William* Gabbitas,

With due respect I would like to draw your attention that at present, I am working as an assistant professor in the Department of Engineering, Islamic University, Kushtia-7003, Bangladesh. I am *highly* interested in continuing my further studies in the field of reducing fuel emissions. I am therefore, very much interested to continue my higher studies for Ph.D. degree in your university under your supervision. I am sending *herewith* my bio-data *in favor of your kind consideration.*

I would be grateful if you would kindly send me information regarding admission procedures and financial support such as grants available from your government, university, or any other sources.

I would very much appreciate it if you would consider me for a position as your research student.

I am eagerly looking forward to your generous suggestion.

With warmest regards.

Sincerely yours

Hussain Choudhury

The above email might be appropriate for sending to academics who are accustomed to using such formal language themselves. However, a more appropriate version, for example, for sending to a professor in the USA, would be:

Dear Professor Gabbitas

I am an assistant professor in the department of Engineering, at the Islamic University in Bangladesh, where I am doing research into reducing fuel emissions. I would be very interested to continue my studies for a PhD under your supervision. From my CV (see attached) you will see that I have been working on very similar areas as you, and I feel I might be able to make a useful contribution to your team.

I would be grateful if you would kindly send me information regarding admission procedures and any financial support that might be available.

I look forward to hearing from you.

Hussain Choudhury

In any case if it's your first contact with someone, it's generally best to use a formal style, particularly if you are writing to someone in a country whose culture you are not very familiar with. This is especially true of Eastern countries such as Korea and Japan, but even in Europe certain countries (e.g., Germany, Italy) tend to be much more formal than others.

4.5 Be careful of your tone when asking people to do something for you

One of the most common reasons for writing an email is to get someone to do something for you. You are more likely to achieve your aims if you adopt a friendly and positive approach and if you don't sound too direct (i.e., as if you were giving someone an order). Here is an example of a request written in various ways from very direct (using an imperative) to overly cautious and extremely polite. You can choose the one you feel is the most appropriate:

Revise the manuscript for me.

Will you revise the manuscript for me?

Can you revise the manuscript for me?

Could you revise the manuscript for me?

Would you mind revising the manuscript for me?

Do you think you could revise the manuscript for me?

Would you mind very much revising the manuscript for me?

If it's not a problem for you could you revise the manuscript for me?

If you happen to have the time could you revise the manuscript for me?

When you translate from your own language into English, you may lose the sense of politeness that the version in your own language had. Thus, it is possible that an email that sounds courteous in your language might sound quite rude when translated into English.

Another problem is that when you write in English, you may be less worried about how your email might be interpreted than you would if you were writing to a colleague of your own nationality. For many non-native speakers, writing in English is like writing through a filter: the way you write seems to have much less importance than it would if you were writing in your own language.

Below is an email from one co-author of a paper to another co-author.

Here is a first version of the manuscript. Read and check everything: in particular, you have to work on the introduction and prepare Fig 1.

You should send it back to me by the end of this month at the latest.

I ask you to suggest also some referees that would be suitable for reviewing the paper.

The above email was written by an Italian researcher to her Canadian co-author. If this email were translated into Italian, it would sound absolutely fine, and the recipient would have no reason to be offended. But in English it sounds like a series of orders given by someone very high in a hierarchy. Thus, the Canadian co-author might have been a little surprised or offended by the tone. The problems are due to the use of

> the imperative (*read and check*)—this gives the impression that the sender is not a co-author on a equal level to the recipient, but rather quite an aggressive professor giving instructions to a student

> *have to*—this sounds like a strong obligation rather than a request

> *should*—again, this sounds like an order

The email could be improved as follows:

> Here is a first version of the manuscript. Please could you read and check everything. In particular, it would be great if you could complete / revise the introduction and also prepare Figure 1.

> Given that our deadline is the first week of next month, I would be grateful to receive your revisions by the end of this month.

> The editor might ask us to suggest some referees to review our paper, so if you have any ideas please let me know.

However, when you are giving a formal list of instructions these will generally be quicker and easier to follow in the form of imperatives (i.e., the infinitive form of the verb without *to*). So the first rather than the second sentence below would be more appropriate in a list of instructions:

> Attach your application form to your email.

> The application form should be attached to the email.

This approach will not be rude

- if you have a friendly introductory phrase before a list of commands

- if the rest of the mail is friendly

If in doubt, use *please.*

4.6   Show your recipient respect and motivate them to reply

Poor spelling and text message writing may not be acceptable to many recipients. They tell the recipient "I am sorry but I could not be bothered to find 30 seconds to check my spelling or to write words in their full form because I have more important things in my life." Below is an email I received from a student I had taught the previous year.

Subject: hlep with cv

Hi pfof Wallwoark

how r u? do u remember me? u said in your lessons that we could send u r cvs for correction. in attachment is mine. pls I need it for tommorow nigth if poss. thankx u.

You need to change your email writing style depending on who you are writing to (their age, position, nationality). Also, just because a professor may have been informal and friendly, it does not mean that you should write to him / her in a casual way. A more suitable version would be:

Subject: help with CV

Dear Professor Wallwork

I attended your scientific papers course last year. I am the student from Russia who told you about Russian writing style. I was wondering whether you might have time to correct my CV (see attached). Unfortunately, I need it for tomorrow - my professor only told me about it today. I know it is asking a lot but if you could find 10 minutes to correct it, I would really appreciate it.

Please let me know if you need any further information about how Russian academics write.

Best wishes

The revised request is better because:

- it reminds me who he is and that he once did a favor for me

- the student acknowledges that his request may be asking me "a lot" but he shows his appreciation of what I might be able to do for him

- he offers to return the favor

Clearly, there does not need to be an exchange of favors. The email could have been written as follows:

> Subject: help with CV
>
> Dear Professor Wallwork
>
> I attended your scientific papers course last year - it was really useful and since then I have had two papers published. Thank you!
>
> I seem to remember that during your course you offered to correct our CVs for us.
>
> So although it is a year later, I was wondering whether you might have time to correct my CV (see attached). Unfortunately, I need it for tomorrow - my professor only told me about it today. I know it is asking a lot but if you could find 10 minutes to correct it, I would really appreciate it and I am sure it would make a significant difference to my chances of getting the post.
>
> Thank you very much in advance.

4.7 Use common interests to establish and cement a relationship

When you call someone on the phone, you probably begin by asking *how are you?*. You are not necessarily interested in the answer, but it is just a formality at the beginning of a phone call. Some people also ask this question at the start of an email—again they may not be expecting an answer, but it just acts as a friendly start rather than being too direct.

If you have a good relationship with your recipient, then they are more likely to carry out your requests and do so more quickly than they might if you are totally anonymous to them. My tactic after a few email exchanges is to reveal / announce some personal information.

This could be at the beginning of the email, for instance:

> Hope you had a good weekend. I spent most of mine cooking.
>
> So how was your weekend? We went swimming—we were the only ones in the sea!
>
> How's it going? I am completely overloaded with work at the moment.

Or it could be the end of the email:

> Ciao from a very hot and sunny Pisa.
>
> Hope you have a great weekend—I am going to the beach.

These little exchanges only take a few seconds to write (and to be read, i.e., by the recipient). Also, by making comments such as these, you might discover that you have something in common (cooking, swimming), and this will give you something to "talk" about in your emails.

I have found that such exchanges "oil" the relationship. Also, if in the future there are any misunderstandings, then these are likely to be resolved more quickly and with a better outcome than there might be with an anonymous interlocutor.

However, it is really important not to take this to extremes. One of my colleagues complained that a student, who she hardly knew, began his email to her saying:

> I saw your status on Facebook. It seems you had a nice time in Venice!

Although Facebook is public and was specifically designed to let people into your private life (or at least that part of your private life that you want them to have access to), some users of Facebook find the idea of people who they hardly know looking at their pages and then commenting on them as being quite distasteful. It is a bit like being stalked. So, be careful to respect people's privacy and not be invasive.

4.8 Maintain a friendly relationship

Whenever you write an email, always be aware that there is probably more than one way to interpret what you have written and that this other way may cause offence. So, before you send your email, check for potential misinterpretations, and rewrite the offending phrase.

For example, here is what appears to be an inoffensive reminder.

> For your reference I remind you that it is VERY important to always specify your current workstation IP address.

However, this sentence has various problems:

- *For your reference* could be interpreted as sounding like someone who has been contradicted and is now giving their point of view in quite an aggressive way

- *I remind you*—the present tense in English is sometimes used to give a sense of authority or formality. It thus sounds very cold and unfriendly

- *VERY*—rather than using capitals, consider using bold. Also, it sounds rather like a teacher talking to a naughty (badly behaved) child

Here are two different ways of rewriting the sentence:

Just a quick reminder—don't forget to specify your current workstation IP address. Thanks!

I'd just like to remind you that the IP address of a workstation must always be specified.

The first alternative is informal and friendly. The second is more formal, but uses three tricks to make it soft:

1. a contracted form (*I'd* rather *than I would*) which gives the phrase a less authoritarian tone

2. the passive form—this then makes the *IP address* the subject of *specified* (rather than the implicit *you must specify*)

3. *a workstation* rather than *your workstation*—this makes the message sound that it is not directed personally at the recipient

4.9 Adopt a non-aggressive approach

If you have something negative to say, it is advisable not to adopt an aggressive approach (see Chapter 10). Aggression is more likely to aggravate the situation than solve it. Compare:

AGGRESSIVE	NON-AGGRESSIVE
You have sent us the wrong manuscript.	You appear to have sent us the wrong manuscript.
	It seems we've been sent the wrong manuscript.
I need it now.	I appreciate that this is a busy time of year for you but I really do need it now.
I have not received a reply to my email dated ...	I was wondering whether you had had a chance to look at the email I sent you dated ... (see below)

When you revise your email before hitting the "send" button, make sure you remove anything that is not strictly necessary, particularly phrases that might annoy the recipient. Recipients do not like to be treated like schoolchildren or be made to feel guilty; thus, in most contexts the phrases below should be deleted:

This is the second time I have written to request …

I am still awaiting a response to my previous email …

As explained in my first email,

As clearly stated in my previous email,

In summary: Use a more roundabout, softer approach and include an introductory phrase that in some way tones down any aggression. If possible empathize with your reader's situation.

4.10   Add a friendly phrase at the end of an email

There are various phrases that you can use at the end of an email, particularly if you think the rest of the email may be a little strong. These include the following:

Have a nice day.

Have a great weekend.

Keep up the good work.

4.11 An example of how a simple and friendly request can lead to a possible collaboration

Below is a string of emails between one of my students, Katia Orlandi, and the author of a paper, Olaf Christensen. As usual, I have changed their names and some details for reasons of privacy. Note how

- the string of emails becomes less and less formal

- they quickly build up a good relationship by showing interest in each other's work and countries

- they end up with a potential collaboration

Dear Dr. Christensen,

I'm a PhD Student at the Department of Engineering, at the University of Pisa in Italy.

I am doing research into energy-saving solutions for p2p overlay networks (e.g., Red BitTorrent).

I'm writing to you because I'm interested in your paper:

J. Breakwater and O. Christensen, "Red BitTorrents? The answer to everything".

I would appreciate it very much if you could send me a copy by email. By the way, I have found your previous papers really interesting; they have been a great stimulus to my research.

Thanks in advance.

Regards

Katia Orlandi

Hello Katia

Attached is our paper which we are going to present at the Fifth International Workshop on Red Communications next June.

I see you are from Pisa … a small but beautiful city. I have been there (to see the Leaning Tower, of course).

Let me know if you have any questions about the BitTorrent work.

Olaf

Dear Dr. Christensen,

Thank you so much for your quick reply. I have already read half the paper - really useful.

Yes, Pisa is a great city, though I am actually from Palermo in Sicily. I see you work in Denmark; I was in Copenhagen this summer; it was really beautiful.

I am actually going to the Red Communications conference too! It would be great to meet up.

Ciao

Katia

Hi Katia

Out of curiosity I looked you up on your webpage at your department's website. You seem to have done a lot of research in the same area as our time. I was wondering whether you might be interested in working on a new project that my prof and I are setting up. In any case, let's arrange to meet at the Red C conference … By the way, it's Olaf, I am not used to being addressed as Dr. Christensen :).

Chapter 5
Language, Translating and Spelling

Factoids

The European Commission (EC) was one of the pioneers of machine translation and at one time their translation service produced over one million pages per year. About one third of the officials working in the European Union's (EU) institutions were once employed in connection with interpretation and translation. The cost of translation now accounts for around 1% of the EU budget. At the time of writing, the EU has 24 official and working languages. Originally all EU documents were translated into the language of the member countries, now to due time and money constraints only a few have this privilege. According to the EC Multilingualism website, the most multilingual EU citizens are the Luxembourgers, where 99% of people know at least one other foreign language, followed by Slovaks (97%), and Latvians (95%).

*****

Esperanto (meaning one who hopes) was a language devised by Dr Lazar Zamenhof who was born in 1859 in Białystok, which at the time was in Russia but is now in Poland. Zamenhof felt that there could only be peace in the world if everyone spoke the same language so that no one would have a cultural advantage over anyone else. He published his work in 1887, during a period in which another 53 artificial universal languages were created. Esperanto has its own Wikipedia site – Vikipedio (eo.wikipedia.org), and Esperanto congresses are held every year. According to Wikipedia, the number of current speakers is estimated at between 250 and 5000.

*****

One of the most infamous translations of all time was a book entitled *New Guide of the Conversation in Portuguese and English*. This book of familiar phrases had originally been published in 1836 in French and Portuguese. When an English version was produced, the services of Pedro Carilino were used. Carilino understood no English at all and merely used a French-English dictionary. The resulting book informed readers that a relation was for male relations (e.g. fathers, uncles) and an relation for female relations. In fact, he used a for masculine words, and an for feminine words throughout his guide. Carilino concluded his book by saying: We expect then, who the little book (for the care that we wrote him, and for her typographical correction) that may be worth the acceptation of the studious persons, and especially of the Youth, at which we dedicate him particularly.

*****

Google Translate was introduced in 2007, initially with translations from French, German and Spanish into English, and vice versa.

© Springer International Publishing Switzerland 2016
A. Wallwork, *English for Academic Correspondence*,
English for Academic Research, DOI 10.1007/978-3-319-26435-6_5

5.1 What's the buzz?

Discuss these questions.

1. How important is it to write correct English in an email? Is it less important than in a research paper?

2. Are readers more accepting of mistakes in an email? If so, does it mean that it is OK to make mistakes?

3. Compared to other forms of writing (e.g. reports, articles, essays, form filling) does email make use of more or fewer standard phrases? What are the implications of this?

4. What are the dangers of using Google Translate to translate from your language into English or to check that your English is correct?

****

This chapter is designed to help you:

- minimize the number of mistakes that you make in English

- understand the importance of writing in a clear, simple, unambiguous manner

- be aware of the dangers of using Google Translate … and also the benefits

- remember to check your spelling

5.2 Minimize mistakes in your English by writing short and simple emails

Keep your emails short and simple.

The following are two versions of an email from a French student who wishes to do an internship at another institute.

ORIGINAL VERSION (OV)

Dear Professor Gugenheimer,

I am Melanie Duchenne, the french student who Holger Schmidt told you about few days ago.

Firstly, I would like to thank you for the opportunity you afford me to spend with your staff a short period, which would be extremely useful for me in order to obtain the master degree.

I have been adviced by Holger to communicate to you my preference as soon as possible, and I beg your pardon for not having done it earlier, due to familiar problems. Then, if possible, the best option for me would be a two-months period, from the beginning of june to the end of july. Waiting for your reply, I wish to thank you in advance for your kindness.

Best regards,

Melanie Duchenne

REVISED VERSION (RV)

Dear Professor Gugenheimer,

I am the French student who Holger Schmidt told you about.

Firstly, I would like to thank very much you for the opportunity to work with your team.

If possible, the best option for me would be June 1 – July 31.

I apologize for not letting you know the dates sooner.

Best regards,

Melanie Duchenne

The RV is much more concise and precise. All non-essential information (from the recipient's point of view) has been removed. Reducing the amount of text reduces the number of mistakes. Below are the mistakes in the OV, with the correct version on the right.

few days ago = a few days ago

the opportunity you afford me = the opportunity you are giving me

obtain the master degree = to get my Master's [degree]

I have been adviced = I have been advised by Holger *or* Holger advised me

familiar problems = family problems

a two-months period = a two-month period

All of the above mistakes have been removed, simply by reducing the amount of the text.

Note also the correct capitalization (*Prof, French, Best*) in the RV.

5.3 Don't experiment with your English, instead copy / adapt the English of the sender

The less you write, the fewer chances you have of making mistakes with your English.

Imagine you have received an email whose closing line is:

If we don't speak before, I hope you have a Happy Christmas!

You can limit the number of mistakes you could potentially make by repeating part of the sender's greeting:

Happy Christmas to you too!

Do not experiment and try to translate what you might have written in your own language, for example:

Let me express my warmest wishes to you and your family for a very happy Christmas and a New Year full of both personal and professional gratifications.

The above Christmas greeting is four times longer than the original Christmas greeting—the potential for making mistakes in English is thus substantially higher. The long greeting has two problems:

- It is extremely formal compared to the rest of the email and thus sounds a little out of place

- It is probably a literal translation of what Raul would have said if he had been writing in his own language—however, the last part of the sentence (*full of both personal and professional gratifications*) does not exist in English (a Google search does not give any hits)

Copying the phrase of the sender and / or adding *too* is a good tactic for repeating a greeting, as the following examples highlight (the sender's greeting is on the left, the recipient's reply on the right):

I hope you have a great weekend.	I hope you have a great weekend too.
Have a great weekend.	You too.
Enjoy your holiday.	I hope you enjoy your holiday too.

Not all phrases can be replied to simply by adding *too*. For example, if the sender writes *See you next week at the meeting*, you cannot reply with *See you next week too*. Instead, you could write *I am looking forward to seeing you at the meeting* or *Yes, I am looking forward to it* or *I am looking forward to seeing you again*.

5.4 Be concise and precise

Below are some examples of words and phrases that are typically used to introduce new concepts or link sentences together. For example, the following phrases could all be replaced with *because*:

because of the fact that

due to the fact that

in consequence of

in the light of the fact that

in view of the fact that

And these could be replaced with either *although* or *even though*:

in spite of the fact that

regardless of the fact that

However, do not confuse conciseness with brevity (i.e., using the minimum number of words). Brevity may have two major disadvantages:

- lack of precision and clarity

- it may sound rude and suggest that you couldn't find the time to make yourself polite and clear

For guidelines on how to be concise, see Chapter 5 in the companion volume *English for Writing Research Papers.*

5.5   Use short sentences and choose the best grammatical subject

A lot of research has shown that when native English speakers read, their eyes tend to focus at the beginning and end of the sentence, whereas the middle part of the sentence tends to be read more quickly.

The way we read today is also very different from the way we read until the mid-1990s. The Internet encourages us to read very quickly—this is known as browsing, scanning, or skimming. Because we want information fast in order to help us decide whether to respond to an email and what action to take, we tend not to read every word. Instead we skip from word to word, sentence to sentence, and paragraph to paragraph until we find information that we consider useful or important. If we don't find anything of value, we stop reading.

Essentially, you need to

- select the most important item to put as the grammatical subject of the sentence

- put the verb and object as close as possible to the subject

- limit yourself to a sentence with two parts—so that there is only a beginning part and an end part. If you have three parts (or more), the middle parts will be read with less attention

The sentence below is a 48-word sentence written by a female PhD student. It contains three parts. It is not hard to read.

> I am a PhD student in psycholinguistics and one of the professors in my department, Stavros Panageas, kindly gave my your name as he thought you might be able to provide me with some data on the use of the genitive in Greek dialects of the 17th century.

Nevertheless it requires more effort than this alternative:

> Your name was given to me by Professor Stavros Panageas. I am doing a PhD on the use of
> the genitive in Greek. Prof Panageas told me you have a database on 17th century Greek
> dialects and I was wondering if I might have access to it.

The first sentence of the alternative version now has *your name* as the subject rather
than *I am*. This means that the recipient sees himself / herself as the most important
topic, and the sender thus takes second place. The second sentence then explains who
the sender is and indicates her research area (which coincides with that of Prof
Panageas). In the third sentence Prof Panageas is the subject of the sentence, not
because he is the most important element in the sentence, but only because it would
be unnatural to make *17th century Greek dialects* the subject. Thus, the three parts of
the original sentence have become three separate sentences in the revised version.

Having short sentences

- helps your recipients locate the key information in your sentence with the
  minimal mental or visual effort

- makes it much easier for you to delete parts of your email or add parts to it.
  For example, if the sender realizes that her email is too long, she could easily
  delete the phrase *I am doing a PhD on the use of the genitive in Greek* in the
  alternative version. Deleting *I am a PhD student in psycholinguistics* in the
  original version would mean that the rest of the sentence would also have to
  be modified for it to make sense

5.6   Use the correct word / phrase order

Structuring your sentence by putting the words in the their most logical (as well as
grammatical) order is key to writing an effective email. See 15.19 and Chapter 2 in
the companion volume *English for Writing Research Papers*.

The examples sentences below are not written following the natural word order of
English.

> Your paper, which was sent to me by Wolfgang Froese, a colleague of mine at the XTC lab
> in Munich, was extremely useful and I would like…

> Our manuscript, owing to some difficulties with our equipment due an electrical black out
> caused by the last hurricane, will be delayed.

The two sentences above both contain parenthetical phrases, that is, a phrase which separates the subject (*paper, manuscript*) from its verb (i.e., *was, will be delayed*). When someone reads an email, they want to be able to absorb the information as quickly and as easily as possible. Recipients are generally not prepared to devote the same attention to reading an email as they might to a paper. Here are possible rewritten versions of the two sentence above:

> Your paper was sent to me by Wolfgang Froese, a colleague of mine at the XTC lab in Munich. I found it extremely useful and I would like...

> I am writing to inform you that unfortunately our manuscript will be delayed. The delay is due to...

Using the same word order as you would if you were speaking does not mean that your email should sound like someone is talking—it still has to be well organized and all redundancy removed. It means writing in a way that is "recipient friendly": short, simple sentences with minimal need for punctuation (i.e., no parenthetical phrases divided off by commas).

Finally, be careful of the location of the word *please* as it can give a very different tone to the sentence.

> Please can you let me know as soon as possible. (neutral)

> Hugo please note that... (neutral)

> Please Hugo, note that... (irritated)

Please is not usually followed by a comma.

5.7 Avoid ambiguity

You should make sure that you give an email the same attention as any other important written document by making it 100% clear and unambiguous. If you don't, it can be annoying for the recipient, who is often forced to ask for clarifications.

Ambiguity arises when a phrase can be interpreted in more than one way, as highlighted by these examples:

The student gave her dog food. Does "her" refer to the student (i.e., it is the student's dog), or is "her" another person to whom the student gave dog food?

You can't do that. Does *can't* mean that it would be impossible for you to do that, or that you don't have permission to do that?

Our department is looking for teachers of English, Spanish, and Chinese. Is the department looking for three different teachers (one for each language), or one teacher who can teach all three languages?

The older professors and students left the lecture hall. It is not clear if "older" just refers to the professors or to the students as well.

I like teaching students who respect their professors who don't smoke. Who are the non-smokers, the professors or the students?

Each subscriber to a journal in Europe must pay an additional $10. Is the journal a European journal, or do the subscribers live in Europe?

For more on this topic, see Chapter 6 in the companion volume *English for Writing Research Papers.*

5.8 When using pronouns ensure that it is 100% clear to the recipient what noun the pronoun refers to

A common problem in emails is the use of a pronoun (e.g., *it, them, her, which, one*) that could refer to more than one noun. The sentences in the first column below have been disambiguated in the third column.

AMBIGUOUS SENTENCE	REASON FOR AMBIGUITY	POSSIBLE DISAMBIGUATION
Thank you for your email and the attachment *which* I have forwarded to my colleagues.	*which*—email? attachment? or both?	Thank you for your email. I have forwarded the *attachment* to my colleagues.
To download the paper, you will need a user name and password. If you don't have *one*, then please contact…	*one*—user name? password? or both?	To download the paper, you will need a user name and password. If you don't have a *password*, then please contact…
Yesterday I spoke to Prof Jones, and on Tuesday I saw Prof Smith and one of his PhD students, Vu Quach. If you want, you can write to *them* directly. You will find their emails on the website.	*them*—Smith and Vu? all three people (Jones, Smith, and Vu)?	Yesterday I spoke to Prof Jones, and on Tuesday I saw Prof Smith and one of his PhD students, Vu Quach. If you want you can write to *all three of them* directly.
After a student has been assigned a tutor, *he / she* shall…	*he / she*—the student? the tutor?	After a student has been assigned a tutor, the student shall…

As highlighted in the third column you can avoid ambiguity if you replace pronouns with the nouns that they refer to.

5.9 Use standard phrases rather than translations from your own language

Every language has certain phrases that cannot be translated literally into another language. A high percentage of the content of emails is made up of such standard phrases. You need to be very aware of what these standard phrases are, and what their equivalents are in English—see Chapter 14. You could create your own personal collection of useful phrases, which you can cut and paste from emails written by native English speakers (which hopefully will be correct!).

If you make literal translations into English, the result may sound strange or even comical and thus sound unprofessional. Here are some examples:

GERMAN	JAPANESE	RUSSIAN
Beautiful greetings.	To omit the greetings.	Healthy
I feel pleasure for myself from you to hear.	Thank you for supporting us always.	Wish a success.
Say you a greeting to your wife.	Please kindly look after this.	Calm night.

Using standard phrases enables you to be sure that at least the beginnings and ends of your emails are correct! Then in the body of the email it is advisable not to experiment too much with your English.

English-speaking researchers in the West tend to be less deferential to their professors and use considerably less salutations at the end of an email. An expression such as *Sincerely yours* that might be considered perfectly acceptable by Indian speakers of English sounds much too formal or even rather archaic to someone in the UK or US, where even *Yours sincerely* tends to be reserved for very formal letters. A much more typical salutation is *Best regards*, which works both in formal and more neutral situations.

Note that the use of English varies from one English-speaking country to another. If you are a researcher from India, Pakistan, Bangladesh, and other countries (e.g., in Africa) with strong historical ties to England, then your standard English usage may be considerably more formal than, for instance, in the UK and the US.

Below are some examples from Indian English that might sound a little strange to non-Indians:

If my profile, prima facie matches with your requirements for a summer Intern, please revert back, so that I could furnish any more relevant information.

Looking forward to a reply in the affirmative.

5.10   Don't exaggerate or sound insincere

Here is an extract for a request for an internship. Professors in the West might find the language too formal, exaggerated or insincere, particularly the parts in italics. In addition, the two paragraphs seem to say practically the same thing.

> I am interested in doing a summer internship under your guidance in *your esteemed organization* from May–July next year with the intention of enhancing my knowledge and exploring *my academic and intellectual interest* so as to prepare myself for doctoral study in that particular subject.
>
> My purpose of writing to you is to obtain a creative, challenging and motivating internship in your research group and I am interested to pursue my summer internship under your guidance, where I can utilize my scientific and technological skills to the fullest. I am aware of the *superior quality of research work* at your institute.

Finally, there is nothing in the above email to show that it was written for the specific recipient. It sounds like the same email was sent to several summer school organizers. This kind of 'spammed' email is unlikely to achieve its objective.

5.11   Beware of the potential dangers of Google Translate

Google Translate (GT) is a fantastic tool for rapidly writing documents in another language. The language of emails is very particular because it contains many set phrases (i.e. standard phrases), not all of which Google translates correctly – though the service is constantly improving.

You might like to try the following experiment and see if it works for you:

- Write your email directly into Google Translate.

- Write the salutations directly in English – limit yourself to writing 'Dear ...' at the beginning, and 'Best regards' at the end.

- Write any other phrases that you know are correct directly into English.

- Don't experiment by getting Google to translate set phrases from your language – there is a strong risk that the result will not only be wrong but will also sound ridiculous.

- Write other phrases in your own language but using the simplest form possible, with short sentences.

Even if you use a mix of two languages GT will transform the entire email into uniform English.

Below is an example of what Silvio, an Italian researcher, wishes to write to his colleague Peter. Note that he has written in a mixture of English and Italian, which he then subjects to Google Translate.

Translate from: English

Below is how GT translated the above text.

When you have GT's translation, paste it into your email. Then check it.

In the case above there is a mistake 'control my slide', which in correct English should be 'check my slides'. The reason for this mistake with *control* is that the Italian verb *controllare* (like the equivalents in all Romance languages) can be translated either with *control* or *check* (and GT cannot know which one is correct).

The reason for *slide* being left by GT in the singular is because the word *slide* is also used in Italian, but it has only one form which is both singular and plural.

I thank you would also be better translated simply as *Thank you*. In this case, Silvio could have deleted the phrase altogether, or simply written *Thanks*.

So:

- check for vocabulary mistakes

- ensure that English words that are used in your native language are used in their correct form in their translated version

- paraphrase or delete any phrases that you are not 100% sure of

- write directly into English any standard phrases that you know are correct

In any case, even if Silvio had sent Peter the GT version with no corrections, Peter would have understood the message without any difficulty.

In my own tests with my students, I have found that GT tends to make fewer mistakes than students do when they translate 'manually'. In addition, some of the mistakes that GT makes are very obvious, so they are easy to spot.

5.12   Be careful how you use pronouns

Unlike most languages, English uses the same word *you* for everyone. It is not possible to show more respect by capitalizing the *y* (i.e., *You*, *Your*)—this form does not exist in English. Thus, the phrase below is incorrect:

> I believe Your paper would help me in my research. Thank You in advance for any help You may be able to give me.

Christopher Robin, a character in A. A. Milnes' famous stories about Winnie the Pooh, said:

> If the English language had been properly organized … then there would be a word which meant both "he" and "she," and I could write, "If John or Mary comes, heesh will want to play tennis," which would save a lot of time.

In modern English this problem has been resolved by using "they." In Anglo countries there are some rules regarding the use of politically correct language which help to make the communication more neutral and avoid the likelihood of offending anyone.

The masculine pronoun should not be used to refer to a generic person who is not necessarily or specifically a man.

GENERALLY INCORRECT	CORRECT
Someone called for you but *he* didn't leave *his* name.	Someone called but *they* didn't leave *their* name.
This should enable the user to locate *his* files more easily.	This should enable *the user* to locate *his / her* files more easily. This should enable *users* to locate *their* files more easily.

As can be seen from the examples:

- *they / their* can be used with reference to singular subjects (e.g., *someone*, *a person*, *some guy*)

- *he / she* and *his / her* can be used as an alternative to *he* and *his*

The simplest solution is often to make the subject plural and then use *they* and *their*.

5.13   Check your spelling and grammar

The email below is a request for an internship.

Dear Prof Caroline Smiht,

I am student at the department of biology who is working with Professor Ihsan (Vibravoid Project). How You probably remember, I asked to You to have the opportunity of spending a period at the Your lab in Toronto. What I'd know is if I can still came to Your lab, in order to confirm the acomodation I have found in Toronto.

Waiting for Your replyThank you in advance,

Boris Grgurevic

PS I have booked my flights to get cheap ones

The above email is a disaster. First, the sender misspells the professor's name (*Smiht* instead of *Smith*). This will instantly put the professor in a negative frame of mind and will not help her to be receptive to the request. Second, it contains many mistakes in English, spelling, capitalization (e.g., *You* instead of *you*) and layout.

It is essential that you check your English and particularly your spelling. Mistakes create a very poor impression on your recipient who may think "if this person cannot take the time to check their spelling then they might have the same approach to not checking their data."

A more acceptable version would be:

Dear Professor Smith,

We met last month when you were doing a seminar at the Department of Biology in *name of town*. I am a student of Professor Ihsan (Vibravoid Project). You mentioned it might be possible for me to work at your lab for two months this summer.

I was wondering if the invitation is still open, if so would June to July fit in with your plans? My department will, of course, cover all my costs.

I would be grateful if you could let me know within the next ten days so that I will still be in time to book cheap flights and get my accommodation organized.

I look forward to hearing from you.

5.14   Don't rely 100% on your spell checker

As you can see from the poem below, spell checkers will only find words, or rather, combinations of letters, that do not exist.

Eye halve a spelling chequer	I have a spelling checker
It came with my pea sea	It came with my PC
It plainly marques four my revue	It plainly marks for my review
Miss steaks eye kin knot sea.	Mistakes I cannot see.
As soon as a mist ache is maid	As soon as a mistake is made
It nose bee fore two long	It knows before too long
And eye can put the error rite	And I can put the error right
Its rarely ever wrong.	It's rarely ever wrong.

This means that your spell checker would not find any of the mistakes in the following email.

Tanks for your male, it was nice to here form you. I was glad to no that you are steel whit the Instituted of Engineering and that they still sue that tool that I made for them, do they need any spare prats for it? I am filling quite tried, tough fortunately tomorrow I'm going a way for tow weeks—I have reversed a residents in the Bahamas!

That's all fro now, sea you soon.

Of course, even if your email is full of spelling mistakes, most people will be able to read it, as the extract below proves. However, you will give a poor image of yourself.

The phaonmneal pweor of the hmuan mnid. Aoccdrnig to rscheearch at Cmabrigde Uinervtisy, it deosn't mttaer in waht oredr the ltteers in a wrod are, the olny iprmoatnt tihng is taht the frist and lsat ltteer be in the rghit pclae. The rset can be a taotl mses and you can sitll raed it wouthit a porbelm. Tihs is bcuseae the huamn mnid deos not raed ervey lteter by istlef, but the wrod as a wlohe. Amzanig huh? yaeh and I awlyas thought slpeling was ipmorantt!

5.15 If the mail is very important, have it checked by an expert

If your career in some way depends on the email, then ensure you have it revised by a native English speaker.

Chapter 6

Requests and Replies

Factoids

The top 10 words most commonly used words in English are: *the, of, and, a, to, in , is, you, that, it.*

The 199th most commonly used word in English is *America*, which is the only country in the top 300, though *Indian* is 283rd. *World* is number 200.

Mother (192) comes before *father* (213) and *children* (253). But *he* (11) is more than four times more commonly used than *she* (46), and *boy* (141) is twice as common as *girl* (288).

Man and *men* are ranked 124 and 168, but *woman* (ranked 762) and *women* are not even on the list of the top 300 (though words such as *animal, car, important, oil, list* and *plant* are).

The first person singular pronoun *I* is at number 20 *and* my at 81, which is after *his* (18) and *her* (62).

The three most common verbs are: *be* (22), *have* (24), and *can* (39).

Apart from numerals and possessive adjectives, the most commonly used adjectives are: *long* (92) and *new* (102).

Time (68) comes before *day* (94) and *night* (258).

Unsurprisingly, *first* (83) comes before *second* (274); *paper* (245) before *book* (270); *home* (173) before *house* (188); and *play* (183) before *study* (195) and *learn* (197).

Surprisingly, *English* doesn't make the top 300.

© Springer International Publishing Switzerland 2016
A. Wallwork, *English for Academic Correspondence*,
English for Academic Research, DOI 10.1007/978-3-319-26435-6_6

6.1   What's the buzz?

The two email requests below were received by a professor, the first from an ex student, the second from an unknown student from another country. Read the two emails and then discuss the questions:

Request 1

Dear Prof. Skrotun,

Could you please send me a reference letter? I am considering to apply for PhD in Management. As some universities require students to upload a reference letter, I request that you to send me a reference letter as soon as possible.

REQUEST 2

Dear Prof.

I am Amit Khan and I would like to apply for the Master's program in Business Informatics at your esteemed university for next winter semester. I am very much interested in this program. So I hereby send you my passport, CV, degree certificate, academic transcripts, motivational letter.

So, please find the attached documents and do the needful.   Thanking you.

Questions

1. How many emails do you think the average professor receives every day?

2. Do you think professors take pleasure in responding to requests?

3. In the case of the two requests below, how do you think the professor might react?

4. How long do you think it took the students to write their emails?

5. In the second request, which phrases do you think might not exist in the English spoken in the US and UK?

6. How could the emails be improved in order to ensure a response from the professor?

****

Two of the most common types of emails that academics send are (1) requests, and (2) apologies for not having answered a previous email. Many of your requests as an academic may have a big impact on your career—for example, requests for an internship, for a summer school, or for someone to revise your paper. It is thus essential to make your requests clear and concise, as well as quick and easy for your recipient to answer. Equally, when replying to a request, your answers should be precise and easy to understand.

In this chapter you will learn that

- how you structure and specify your request is a strong determinant of whether your request will be met

- intelligent use of numbering and white space can increase the chances of your recipient replying with the correct information

- you should avoid focusing just on your own needs, but also try to understand the recipient's viewpoint

- you can avoid mistakes in English by inserting your replies within the sender's original text

6.2 Lay out your request clearly

Below is a request to register for a conference. Unfortunately, it forces the recipient to read the mail carefully in order to understand exactly what the request is.

Dear Secretariat of the 5th XTC Ph.D. Symposium,

My Supervisor and I would like to register for the XTC Symposium but we couldn't find any registration form in your website. I would be very grateful to you if you could suggest me the best way to register for the event. Moreover, would it be possible to pay the registration fee by credit card? Finally, is the preliminary program available for download?

Thank you very much in advance for you kind cooperation.

Best regards

Here is a better organized version of the above:

Dear Secretariat

Please can you answer the following questions:

1. how can I register for the 5th XTC Ph.D. Symposium?
2. can I pay by credit card?
3. where can I download the preliminary program?

Best regards

Or alternatively, given that you have probably simply been unable to locate the right link and that all your questions could be answered by having access to that link, you could write:

Please can send you me the link for registering for the 5th XTC Ph.D. Symposium. Thanks.

The writer of the email below is a student who has already organized an internship in a university in the USA. He is now dealing with the secretary who is helping him with various bureaucratic procedures in preparation for his visit.

Dear Ms Jackson,

I apologize for my late reply, at the moment I am still waiting for the funding letter. Please find attached to this e-mail the DS 20-19 form, duly filled in with all my personal details. As far as the copy of my passport is concerned, I am sending you a copy of my old one, but please note that I need to apply for a new electronic passport complying with the US foreign passport requirements. I will send the application for my new passport this week and start with the visa procedure as soon as I can. I will keep you up to date with the progress of my visa application.

I would be grateful if you could provide me some advice on accommodation, since I am now also trying to look for somewhere preferably within walking distance of the department. I hope you have completed the XTC poster, sorry again for my late reply to your last e-mail. I hope this hasn't caused you any problems.

Best regards

The above email is very confused and poor Ms Jackson must be wondering why her boss accepted the student's application for an internship! A more helpful version would be:

Dear Ms Jackson,

I just wanted to update you on my progress with getting all the documents ready.

- DS 20-19 form: see attached.

- Passport: I am attaching a jpg of my passport; however, tomorrow I will apply for a new electronic passport in order to comply with the US foreign passport requirements.

- Visa: I made the application three weeks ago, I hope to have some news by the end of this week.

- Funding letter: I should have this ready early next week - thanks for your patience.

Just a couple of other things: 1) Do you have any suggestions for finding accommodation within walking distance of the department? 2) Did you manage to complete the XTC poster?

Thank you.

I am very sorry it has taken me so long to get back to you, but bureaucracy in my country is a nightmare!

Best regards

The revised version would certainly take the writer about twice as long to write. But in taking this extra time he will impress Ms Jackson with his efficiency and clarity, and he is far more likely to get Ms Jackson's help in his search for accommodation. People are always more willing to help you, if you have clearly shown that you have tried to help them too—in this case the student has helped Ms Jackson perform her work by laying out everything very clearly in his email to her.

6.3 Don't assume that the reader will understand the importance of or reason for your request

When asking someone to cooperate on a project, don't assume that your reader will understand the reasons why they should cooperate with you. Give them a clear list, 'because ..." or any type of request.

Imagine you want one of your co-authors, who also happens to be a native speaker of English, to review the English of your paper.

Simply writing the following email may not be enough:

> Dear Katie
>
> Would you mind reading through the paper and making corrections using 'Track Changes' on Word?
>
> Best regards
>
> Natacha

Compare the above version with the version below:

> I was wondering whether you could do me a favour.
>
> The paper we co-wrote has been accepted for publication, but subject to a review of the English language.
>
> I contacted a professional editing agency, but they want 375 euros to do the job, which to me seems a little excessive.
>
> Would you mind reading through the paper and making corrections using 'Track Changes' on Word?
>
> As you can imagine, research funds here in Spain are very limited, so anything you could do to help would be much appreciated.

The revised version explains

- the situation - paper accepted subject to English review

- what you have done to try to rectify the problem - contacted editing agency

- why your solution failed - too expensive

- request

- why the request is so important

The first line could also have begun: I have some good news - our paper has been accepted for publication! But this might be a rather devious way to convince someone to do something for you.

6.4 Motivate the recipient to reply by empathizing with their situation or by paying them a compliment

Most recipients are more likely to meet your requests if you seem to show some understanding of their situation or if you appreciate their skills in some way. Here are some typical phrases that senders use to motivate their recipients to reply.

I know that you are very busy but ...

Sorry to bother you but ...

I have heard that you have a mountain of work at the moment but ...

Any feedback you may have, would be very much appreciated.

I have an urgent problem that requires your expertise.

I really need your help to ...

I cannot sort this out by myself ...

6.5 Give the recipient all the information they need

When you are making a request asking for a placement in someone's lab, you need to provide your recipient with all the information they need to assess whether there would be benefits for them in having you in their team. The email below is a good example that is likely to motivate the recipient in helping the student to get a placement.

Subject: Laboratory placement - Prof Shankar's student

Dear Professor Janson

I am a PhD student at the University of X. I attended the ACE-Y conference last week and I found your seminar very interesting, the part about the finite element formulation was particularly useful.

I saw on your webpage is it possible to have a placement period in your lab. It would be a real pleasure for me to join your research group and do some further research into the formulation of an efficient finite element for the adhesive layer.

My research covers almost exactly the same topics:

1. FE calculations of complex bonded structures
2. Efficient techniques to reduce d.o.f
3. Enhancing adhesive strength

The area where I think **I could really add value would be in enhancing adhesive strength**. I have attached a paper and some recent results, which I hope you will find both interesting and useful. I believe my approach could work in conjunction with yours and really improve efficiency.

If it would suit you, I could come from April next year, for a 3–6-month period. I would be able to get funding from my university to cover the costs of a placement period, so I need no grant or scholarship.

Please find attached my CV with the complete list of my publications and a letter of recommendation from my tutor, Professor Shankar.

Thank you in advance for any help you may be able to give me.

Mercedes Sanchez Tirana

Mercedes structures her email as follows; she

- explains who is she and how she knows of Janson

- makes a compliment on Janson's seminar

- states why she is writing to Janson

- gives a short summary of her research area highlighting its similarities with Janson's

- highlights where she could add value—she uses bold to attract Janson's attention (he may just be scanning the email to see whether it is worth him reading it)

- says when she is available and that she already has funding

- attaches her CV and other information that provides evidence that she would be a useful addition to Janson's team

- mentions the name of her tutor (who through the literature may be known to Janson)

She also uses a clear subject line which should motivate Janson to open the email.

6.6   Consider not sending an attachment to someone with whom you have had no previous contact

Some people do not appreciate

- receiving attachments from people with whom they have had no previous contact

- long introductory emails

If Mercedes (6.5) wanted to avoid sending an attachment, she could use the same beginning as in her original email up to where she says *really improve efficiency*. Then she could then proceed as follows:

> In addition, I could send you my CV with the complete list of my publications and a letter of recommendation from my tutor, Professor Shankar.
>
> If it would suit you, I could come from April next year, for a 3–6-month period. I would be able to get funding from my university to cover the costs of a placement period, so I need no grant or scholarship.
>
> I look forward to hearing whether you think a collaboration would also be of benefit to you and your team.
>
> Mercedes Sanchez Tirana

With respect to her initial draft, Mercedes has

- removed all references to attachments and simply suggested that she could send him such information

- retained the reference to when she could come and the fact that she needs no funding from Janson

- referred to the possible benefit for Janson and his team

6.7   Include all the relevant information that the recipient needs to assess your request

If you have an important request to make, for example, the one outlined in 4.3, then it is imperative to supply the recipient with all the information that they need in order to assess your request.

An internship could lead to a considerable enhancement in your career possibilities. It is thus wise to give the following information to the person who might be hosting you:

- some details about what you are proposing in terms of scientific content. Also, give the professor other possible areas that you could work on together

- your ideal dates and other dates that you could come

- an indication of whether or not you will be financially autonomous

- a letter of recommendation from your professor

- references from other people

The idea is that it really seems that you want to work with them and that you are trying to make their life easier by providing them with all the information they may want to know.

6.8   When asking someone to review your work, give explicit instructions

When you ask someone to informally review your work, make sure first of all that you do so politely.

Then be 100% explicit exactly what you expect the person to do; you cannot say *Please could you revise my manuscript.* You need to tell them what to focus on, bearing in mind that they may not have time to do a thorough job. Here is an example:

Dear Carlos

I hope all is well with you.

I am currently working on a paper that I would like to submit to the journal's special issue for the conference. The paper is the extension of the work that I presented as a poster during the conference, which I think you saw. The draft is still at quite an early stage, but I would really appreciate your input.

I know that you have a lot of expertise in this area and I am sure my paper would really benefit from your input. In any case, I have what I think are some really important new results, so I hope that you will find this paper of interest too. Obviously, I don't want to take up too much of your time, so perhaps you might just focus on the Discussion and Results. Also, if you could quickly browse through the Literature Cited to make sure I haven't missed any important papers (yours are all there by the way!).

The deadline for submission is on Oct 10, so if you could get your revisions back to me by the end of this month (i.e., September) that would be great.

I do appreciate the fact that you must be very busy, so please do not hesitate to let me know if you don't have the time.

Thank you very much in advance.

Maria

Note how Maria

- gives a brief overview of what kind of paper it is and what stage it is at

- outlines not only the benefit for herself but also a possible benefit for the recipient

- mentions the recipient's *expertise*

- gives the recipient precise details of the parts of the paper that most need the recipient's attention

- informs the recipient when she needs the manuscript return (she avoids using a formal and totally unhelpful expression such as *Please could you return it at your earliest convenience*)

- acknowledges that the recipient may be busy

- gives the recipient the option not to accept her request

The recipient thus has all the information he needs to decide whether to accept or decline the request. He does not need to ask for clarifications.

If you do not know the recipient very well, then you need to ensure that you are not making yourself a problem for the recipient. In such cases you can give them the option to decline your request by saying:

I appreciate that this must be a busy time of year for you, so please feel free to say "no."

I imagine that many people ask you for help in editing their draft manuscripts, so don't hesitate to let me know if you are overloaded with requests.

6.9   Avoid blocks of text and don't force your reader to make sense of everything

In the case below the sender is requesting some product information. However, she is seriously jeopardizing the chances of receiving an answer. In fact, she has written one long block of text containing a considerable amount of information that is of little or no interest to the recipient. The recipient only needs to know the exact details of the sender's request.

Dear InIt Pipes Inc,

I'm Dr Maria Masqueredo and I work as a researcher at the Department of Engineering of the University of *name of place*. I am currently working on a project that entails the use of shape memory alloy tubes and a colleague of mine referred me to your website where I found a few examples that might satisfy my requirements. Essentially, I need shape memory alloy tubes (not superelastic alloys). The transformation temperature is not a critical parameter (Af = 70∞C or more would be adequate). What is really important is that the ratio between the internal diameter, di, and the external diameter, de, must be near the value of 0.7–0.8. The external diameter can be 1.5 mm or more (not exceeding 12 mm). Do you have any product able to satisfy my constraints? Can you send me an estimate for 5 m of your products? By the way I found a mistake in one your product descriptions, under "steel tubes" I think it should say "alloy" rather than "allay."

Thank you in advance for any help you may be able to give me.

Best regards

A better version would be:

Hi

Do you have a shape memory alloy tube with the following characteristics?

1. transformation temperature of Af = 70∞C or more

2. ratio between the internal diameter and the external diameter must be 0.7–0.8

3. external diameter in a range from 1.5 mm to 12 mm

If so, please could send me an estimate for a 5-m tube.

Thanks in advance.

Maria Masqueredo

In the original example above Maria has not thought about the recipient. She has simply written down her thoughts as they came into her head, thus leaving it to the recipient to make sense of everything. If the recipient has the time to deal with the email he / she might answer it, but there is a good chance that he / she will leave it till later or simply delete it on the basis that it is not time-efficient or cost-effective to deal with it.

6.10   Decide whether it might be better just to make one request rather than several

If you have one particular important thing to ask, only ask that one thing. If you have only one request in your email, the recipient will have fewer options—he or she will either ignore your email, or will reply with a response to your request. The fewer options you give your recipient, the more likely you are to achieve what you want.

Generally speaking, when we receive several requests within the same email, we tend to respond to the request or requests that is / are easiest to deal with, and ignore the others.

6.11   For multiple requests, include a mini summary at the end of the email

Many recipients only read the email once. This means that by the end of the email they may have already forgotten any requests that were made at the beginning of the email. Thus, they may respond to only the request/s that they remember or simply the ones that are easiest for them to deal with. This happens even if you have used bullets and used lots of white space to indicate a clear division between your requests.

Two techniques may help you to increase your chances of getting a reply. These techniques are illustrated in the email below.

Dear Dr Suzuki

I hope you had a good summer. I have three short requests that I hope you might be able to help me with.

REQUEST 1

Do you have any openings for PhD students in your laboratory? I have one truly excellent candidate whose CV I have attached. She has a lot of experience in your field and she also speaks some Japanese.

REQUEST 2

When we met before the summer vacation you told me that you were getting some interesting results in your experiments. I was wondering if you had now completed testing and whether you would be willing to share those results with me.

REQUEST 3

At my department we are planning a series of workshops on XYZ in November this year. Given your international reputation and your expertise in the field, I was wondering whether you might be interested in giving a series of seminars. Your travel and accommodation expenses would of course be paid for by my department.

Summary:

1) Internship for PhD student?

2) Your results

3) Seminars in November

I look forward to hearing from you.

The two techniques are as follows:

- precede each request with a number (Request 1, Request 2, etc.) and put the word request in capital letters so it clearly stands out

- provide a summary of all the requests at the end

Generally speaking, you would only need to use one of the two techniques, particularly if the email is reasonably short as in the example above. But if an email is long and requires scrolling by the recipient, then a summary at the end will certainly increase the chances of your recipient answering all your requests. The summary also helps the recipients as they can simply insert their answers under each point of the summary.

6.12   When making multiple requests, ensure that each individual request is clear

Sometimes you do need to make multiple requests in the same email. This is often the case when asking for details about conferences, summer schools, products, etc. In this case, you are not asking someone for something important such as an internship in a top professor's lab, but simply for information which your recipient should be able to provide without too much effort. Thus, it is perfectly legitimate to ask multiple questions. However, unless you lay out and structure your email very carefully, you are unlikely to get answers to all your questions, but probably only to those questions that your recipients can see the most quickly or which require the least effort on their part.

Make your requests absolutely clear.

Here is an email I received from the permissions department of a publisher:

> Please let me know how many copies of the book are being printed, where they will be sold (what territories), and what is the term of license under section 4779.09 of the Revised Code for this book.

There are two problems with this request. First, there are three requests in one sentence. For recipients this is a problem, because they cannot quickly identify the requests when replying to them. Second, it includes the phrase "term of license under section 4779.09 of the Revised Code." This phrase was probably very clear for the sender (i.e., the publisher) because it relates to their field of business, but it meant nothing to me—it was too technical. My choices were (i) try and find out the meaning on the web, (ii) ask for clarification by writing another email, or (iii) just ignore it completely and simply answer the other two questions.

Basically, most recipients will opt for what seems to the easiest solution, which would be the third solution—ignore the request. So if you are making a request, ensure that you phrase it in such a way that your recipient will have no problem understanding it and will thus

- not need to ask for or look for clarification (and thus not waste further time)

- respond to your request, hopefully with the information you wanted

As always, think in terms of your recipient and not of yourself.

A clearer version of the above email could be:

Please could you kindly answer these three questions:

1. how many copies of the book are likely to be printed per year?
2. what territories will they be sold in?
3. what is the term of license for this book (i.e., when will the contract for the book expire)?

The revised version alerts the recipient that there are three requests to answer, and underlines this by using numbered bullets. The first question is also more precise (*per year*), and the third question now includes an explanation of part of the technical phrase and has simply deleted the reference to the section of the Revised Code as being unnecessary.

Clearly, the revised version would take more time to write than the original version, but the benefit is that the writer is more likely to get replies to all three questions.

To ensure that all your requests get answered, it is generally wise to number them and keep them as short as possible.

6.13   Give deadlines

You will increase your chances of people responding to your requests if you give them a specific deadline. This is much more effective than saying *as soon as possible* or *at your earliest convenience*, as these two phrases give no idea of the urgency of the sender.

However, it pays to give them a reasonably short deadline and not too many options. The longer the deadline you give them, the greater the chance that they will simply not remember to fulfill your request. Typical phrases you can use are as follows:

I need it *within* the next two days.

He wants it *by* 11 tomorrow morning at the latest.

I don't actually need it *until* next week, Tuesday would be fine.

I need it some time *before* the end of next week.

Note how the words in italics are used in the context of deadlines.

within	to mention a period of time, which is always indicated by a plural noun (hours, weeks, months).
by	to indicate a specific moment in the future which is the end point of a period of time during which something must be done
until	with negative verb (*I don't need*) to mean "not before"
before	the same as *by*, but *by* can also mean *at*, whereas *before* can only mean "at any point during a period of time"

The difference between *within* and *by* is the same difference as between *for* and *since* with the present perfect. Examples:

He has been here *for* two days.

He has been here *since* yesterday morning.

If you are the receiver of a deadline or if you simply wish to establish your own deadline, then you can use similar phrases. For example, if someone writes to you saying *Could you revise the section as soon as possible.* You can say:

I should be able to get the revisions back to you *by* the end of this month / *within* the next 10 days.

I am sorry but I won't be able to start work on it *until* Monday / *before* next week at the earliest.

6.14   When you receive a reply, be prepared to ask for clarifications

I surveyed native speakers on how they believed that non-natives should correspond by email with them. They provided the following tips:

• Do not take each word in an email as fact - often numbers given are just estimates.

• Ask questions if something appears to be incorrect or if something could have two meanings.

• If someone says something is 'urgent', clarify with them what 'urgent' means.

• Do not take offense if an email is very short and to the point, it does not mean that the writer is impolite.

6.15 In replies to requests consider inserting your answers within the body of the sender's email

There are basically two ways of replying to an email:

- write your reply under the sender's text

- insert your replies within the sender's text

Let's imagine that you are Raul, a Spanish researcher, and that you have a collaboration with Peter, a British researcher. Peter sends you the email below.

Hi Raul

I hope all is well with you. I was wondering if you could do me a couple of favors. Attached are two documents. The first is an Abstract that I would like you to read and hear your comments on. It is actually 50 words over the limit required by the conference organizers, so if you could find any way to remove a few words that would be great. Also attached is the proposal for the request for funding - for some reason I can't find the email addresses of the people in the Research Unit in Madrid, so could you possibly forward it to them? Thanks. Then finally, you mentioned last time we met that you said that you had a useful bibliographical reference that you thought I should look up, do you think you could send it to me. Thanks very much and sorry to bother you with all this.

If we don't speak before, I hope you have a Happy Christmas!

Best regards

Peter

You could decide to write your reply under Peter's text as follows:

VERSION I

Hi Pete

Good to hear from you. Yes, I am happy to read your Abstract and I will try to reduce the word count. I have forwarded the request for funding proposal to the members of the Madrid RU and I put you in cc. Please find below the references I mentioned:

Sweitzer BJ, Cullen DJ, How well does a journal's peer review process function? A survey of authors' opinions (JAMA1994; 272:152–3)

Let me express my warmest wishes to you and your family for a very happy Christmas and a New Year full of both personal and professional gratifications.

Best regards

Raul

Alternatively you could insert your replies into Peter's text:

VERSION 2

>The first is an Abstract that I would like you to read and hear your comments on. It is actually 50 words

>over the limit required by the conference organizers, so if you could find any way to remove a few

>words that would be great.

OK.

>Also attached is the proposal for the request for funding - for some reason I can't find the email

>addresses of the people in the Research Unit in Madrid, so could you possibly forward it to them?

Done.

>Then finally, you mentioned last time we met that you said that you had a useful bibliographic

>references that you thought I should look up, do you think you could send me them. Thanks very much

>and sorry to bother you with all this.

Sweitzer BJ, Cullen DJ, How well does a journal's peer review process function? A survey of authors' opinions (JAMA1994; 272:152–3)

>If we don't speak before, I hope you have a Happy Christmas!

Happy Christmas to you too!

Note that the word *Done* means that Raul has already forwarded the proposal to the RU in Madrid—it means *I have done what you asked me to do*. If he hasn't done so yet, he could write *Will do*.

The advantages of Version 2 are as follows:

1. You can considerably reduce the amount you write and thus the number of potential mistakes. Raul has written only 7 words compared to the 77 words of the first version.

2. You save yourself time in writing and the recipient time in reading.

3. You are more likely to remember to answer all the requests. Also your recipient can see your replies in direct relation to his / her requests.

The only possible disadvantage is that because you write much less it may seem to the recipient that you are in a hurry and want to deal with his / her email as fast as possible—Version 1 is more friendly. However, given the number of emails that people receive and send every day, this is in my opinion a minor consideration.

6.16   Insert friendly comments within the body of the sender's text

You can insert friendly remarks within the body of an email you have received. Let's imagine that you are a researcher who lives and works in Pisa, Italy. You have just been to Prague to give some seminars. The email below is from the Czech person who organized the seminars for you. You have inserted your comments within her email.

>Hi Paolo

>I hope you had a good trip back to Pisa.

Unfortunately there was a three hour delay due to fog, but anyway I got home safely.

>I just wanted to say that it was good to meet you last week. I thought your seminars were very productive.

Thank you. Yes, I was very pleased by the way they went and I was very impressed by the level of knowledge of your students.

>Say hello to Luigi.

I will do. And please send my regards to Professor Blazkova.

Thank you once again for organizing the seminars and I hope to see you again in the not too distant future.

>Best regards

>Hanka

Chapter 7

Cover Letters for Summer Schools, Internships, Placements, Erasmus, PhD / MA / Postdoc Programs

> **Factoids**
>
> 1. A student from Yale once submitted a video version of his CV to the financial services firm UBS. The seven-minute film was forwarded to every investment in Wall Street with subject lines such as "What NOT to do when looking for a banking job".
>
> 2. A survey conducted by Experian revealed that 37% of job seekers had lied about their previous experience, 21% lied about their qualifications, and 19% had not been honest about their current salaries.
>
> 3. A 12-year study of the career paths of over 650 business professionals revealed that one of the most common mistakes in choosing a career was basing choices on aptitudes rather than interests.
>
> 4. In 1998 the buzzword 'elevator statement' was coined, i.e. a summary, in the time it takes to ride an elevator, made by an entrepreneur to a venture capitalist. The reasoning was that someone who cannot explain their company in thirty seconds does not know his/her stuff. Elevator statements are now often used in job interviews to ask neo-graduates what they could offer their potential employer.
>
> 5. In a survey by Powerchex, a UK pre-employment screening company, discrepancies were found in 43% of the job application forms of students from low ranking UK universities (14% in top universities).
>
> 6. According to researchers at the University of Hertfordshire (UK), a successful personal statement when applying for university directly depends on the specific words and phrases used. Top 10 words to include: *achievement, active, developed, evidence, experience, impact, individual, involved, planning, transferable skills*. Top 10 words to avoid: *always, awful, bad, fault, hate, mistake, never, nothing, panic, problems*.

© Springer International Publishing Switzerland 2016
A. Wallwork, *English for Academic Correspondence*,
English for Academic Research, DOI 10.1007/978-3-319-26435-6_7

7.1   What's the buzz?

The following exercises are designed to get you to think about the content and look&feel of various types of cover letters.

1) Below is the cover letter for an application for a job in a multinational company

　　1.   What visual impact might this letter have on the recipient?

　　2.   How effective is the *Dear Sir/Madam* salutation?

　　3.   Where would you begin new paragraphs?

　　4.   How could the information be given in a better order?

　　5.   What evidence has the writer given that she has tailored (personalized) this letter to a specific company rather than just sending the same letter to hundreds of companies?

　　6.   What could be added / removed to give the letter more impact?

　　7.   Is the indentation aesthetically pleasing and effective?

　　　　Dear Sir/ Madam,

　　　　I am have a BSc in Agricultural Engineering from the American University of Beirut (AUB). Regarding my experience, I had two student jobs at two different labs in AUB and followed attended several workshops. I recently completed a "Master of Sciences in Food Quality and chemistry of natural products" at the Mediterranean Agronomic Institute. The Master's program is spread out over two years: the first includes intensive courses in quality control and second is devoted to the development and the drafting of an applied thesis. I have just completed my thesis concerning the quality of wine grapes following a treatment from maturation dehydration in a tunnel. I am currently employed as a medical representative for the promotion of a micro-nutritional supplement for the Swedish laboratories of PLK. I am presently seeking a more challenging career with a well-established local or multinational company such as yours. I wish to devote myself to food quality improvement more than to the marketing of health supplements, which is my current job. I will be very motivated to work and give my best. I'm attaching my latest resume with the letter. I am available for any further information or interview at the contact addresses stated in my resume.

　　　　Sincerely,

2) Below is a letter enquiring about a possible internship in a professor's lab. Will the recipient get a positive impression from this letter and consequently think seriously about offering the student a position? Why? Why not?

　　　　Dear Professor,

　　　　I am Carmine Pine, a PhD student at the University of Atlantis. I am working on spam-recognition software and I have seen on your lab web page that your group is also working on spam recognition. I have seen from your publications record that your lab is very much advanced in this field of science. As I am also working in this field and I am a beginner in this field I would like to come in your lab for a short term training programme to learn new things in this field of science. Details of my education and research experience are mentioned in my CV which is attached with email. Please find attached file.

3) Below is a request for postdoctoral grant.

1. Why is this an effective letter?

2. Underline any useful phrases you find.

3. Is there any other information that you would add?

Postdoctoral grant, EXEGO project

Dear Dr. Jill Cohen

I am very interested in the postdoctoral grant related to the EXEGO project "*Design of a decision matrix to assess the link between selfies and selfish behavior*", with vacancy number: DPW 08–40.

My background is closely related to the field of cognitive selfish behavior. During my Bachelor's studies in Psychology I participated in projects regarding smoking in the presence of young children, unauthorized parking in disabled parking spaces, financial trading, and other non-altruistic behaviors. In addition, my M.Sc. degree focused on *Acts of Neuro-narcissism in Top League Football Players*. During this period I developed a method to assess the level of narcissistic and selfish behaviors among young extremely wealthy people who had suddenly been catapulted into the public eye.

I am currently finishing my Ph.D. in Postmodern Relational Psychology at the School of Advanced Neurological Studies in Manchester (UK). The work I performed during my Ph.D. studies investigated the ego pathway in the Manchester United first team using a transgenic approach. Part of this research was recently published (*Ego pathways as an indicator of selfish behavior in public*. Functional Psychology. 35(7): 606-618). Additionally, I published the results of this work as an oral presentation at the XVI Congress of the Federation of European Psychologists (FEP) held in Tampere, Finland, in August last year.

The topic of the research position you are offering is fully related to the experience I acquired during my M.Sc. and Ph.D. studies. I am confident that my acquaintance with Neurology and Psychology, including the construction of decision matrices, binary vectors, behavior transformations and analysis of the selfish gene, will allow me to successfully perform this project.

I enclose my CV where you can find more details on my research experience.

Best regards,

****

This chapter covers a wide area of academic correspondence including:

- cover letters for job applications
- motivational letters for internships, summer schools, workshops, Erasmus exchanges etc
- applications for PhD and Postdoc programs

Bad examples are provided followed by good templates.

The key idea when writing such letters and applications is to think from the professor's point of view:

- why would they want you in their team
- what differentiates you from others
- what special knowledge you have that could benefit them (you need to find a 'gap' in their research or in the expertise of their team)
- what the cost will be to them, how this cost could possibly be reduced or avoided

To learn more about writing cover letters, reference letters, CVs etc see *Skills in CVs, Resumes and LinkedIn: A Guide to Professional English.*

PART 1: HOW TO STRUCTURE A LETTER

7.2 Begin your letter with a heading to indicate what job you are applying for

A heading immediately tells the reader what your letter is about, for example a job application or a request to participate in a workshop or summer school. The heading should be in bold and centered.

The heading should be an abbreviated version of the position, workshop etc (see examples below).

If the job is advertised on the institute or company's website, make it clear which particular job you are applying for (see below: *Examples for advertised positions*).

If you don't know if the institute or company has any positions available, indicate what kind of job you are looking for (see below: *Examples for non-advertised positions*).

EXAMPLES FOR ADVERTISED POSITIONS:

Workshop on Bio-economics - Brighton 13/14 July.

I would like to apply for a place at the workshop on the Bio-economics of Environmental Sustainment in Urban Areas. I believe that ...

DPhil project on GPS navigation (position ref. 3453/GPS/navi)

Dear Dr. Moon,

I am very interested in the DPhil project that you are proposing on GPS lunar navigation, advertised on your website. My current research focuses on ...

PhD project: "Physiological tolerance of tropical forest invertebrates".

I would like to apply for the PhD project "Physiological tolerance of tropical forest inverte-brates to microclimate change". I am currently ...

Full-time Winter International Program Intern (June newsletter)

I learnt from your newsletter that you are looking for a full-time Winter International Program Intern in your laboratory for January-May of next year. As you will see from the attached CV, I am ...

EXAMPLES FOR UNADVERTISED POSITIONS:

PhD at the Manchester School of Business

Dear Dr Burgess

I would like to apply for the research position at your university …

Placement at the Institute of Animal Ecology

Dear Professor Smith

I am writing about the possibility of a placement, which is a requirement for my Masters in Ecology at Bordeaux.

7.3 Initial salutation

Your initial salutation should be:

- *Dear* + the first name and last name of the person who is most relevant for the position you are looking for (e.g. a human resources manager, a professor's assistant), provided that this person does not have an academic title. If you can't find the name of this person on the institute / company's website, then make a phone call and find out.
- *Dear* + academic title (e.g. *Professor, Dr*) + surname, if you are applying directly to an individual academic.

Always ensure you have the correct spelling of the person's name.

If you are applying for a summer school or workshop, then finding out the name of the relevant person is not necessary. In such cases, the best solution is to have no initial salutation.

7.4   First paragraph (introduction)

As highlighted by the examples in 7.2, begin by saying what position you are interested in. This will entail repeating some of the information given in the heading, but in a more extended form, i.e. the heading should be an abbreviated form of the job / placement you are interested in.

If the person who you are writing to was referred to you by a third person, then indicate who this third person is. For example:

> Your name was given to me by Professor Kahn, who recommended I should write to you with regard to a position as an intern in ....

7.5   Second / third paragraphs

Examples of how to write these paragraphs are given in Part 2 of this chapter. This subsection just summarizes what you should include.

JOB APPLICATIONS, INTERNSHIPS, PHD PROGRAMS, POST DOC POSITIONS

This is the main part of the letter where you explain how your skills and experience directly relate to your application. It must be absolutely clear to the reader that the letter was written specifically for him / her, or his / her institute. So you should highlight how your skills, strengths, objectives, and interests match their institute and the position you are looking for.

Do not talk about the benefits for you of working for them. Instead think about three key skills that you have, and detail how these would be useful for them, i.e. the added value that you would be bringing to their research team. You can present these three skills as bullets.

Apart from specific technical skills, you could mention some of the following:

- ability to work in a team
- professional, pro-active, flexible, punctual with deadlines
- qualifications (put these on CV, but mention the main qualification in the cover letter)
- problem solving skills
- presentation skills
- ability to write manuscripts technical documents
- high level of English

However, you cannot just list the above, you also need to provide examples to substantiate them (see Chapter 9 in *CVs, Resumes and LinkedIn: A Guide to Professional English*).

SUMMER SCHOOLS, WORKSHOPS

Explain why you are interested in the school or workshop. How does it match what you are studying? Try to think of three areas in your academic studies and career which are relevant to the course.

Make it clear that you have chosen the school or workshop for some particular reason, and that this is not just a spam letter that you have written to hundreds of other schools and workshop organizers.

7.6 Closing paragraph

In your closing paragraph you could include one or more of the following:

- say when you are available to start work, when you are free for an interview
- your contact details
- say you are attaching your CV

7.7 Final salutation

Just have one salutation (see 2.7).

The simplest and most international and most neutral final salutation is *Best regards*. Alternatively you can use the more formal *Yours sincerely*. Another way to end is to write: *I look forward to hearing from you.*

7.8 Recognize the importance of such letters and triple check everything

The kinds of letters covered in this chapter could theoretically change your career, particularly those where you apply for an internship or a PhD / Postdoc. You should give them the same importance as you might to conducting a particularly important part of your research.

When you have finished your letter:

- cut any information that will not add explicit value for the recipient
- check that you have not written any English phrases that you are not 100% certain about - if you are not sure they are correct, paraphrase them in a way that you know is correct
- check you have not translated any standard phrases literally into English
- look at the layout - is it clear and simple (all aligned to the left, with no indentations)?
- have you chosen a standard font?
- could some info be better expressed / highlighted as bullets?
- have you double checked the name of the person you are writing to, plus any names of projects and institutes, towns etc?
- have you done a spelling check?

Bear in mind that your recipient (e.g. professor, human resources manager, workshop organizer) will not appreciate any of the following:

- strange (non-standard) email addresses: randy69@hotmail.com, lordofdarkness@death.com
- unclear subject lines
- unclear requests
- multiple emails – i.e. where it is obvious that you have sent the same email to a lot of other people
- advertisements after your signature
- strange fonts and colors
- cut and pastes
- txt mssg style
- too much text
- missing contact details
- spelling mistakes

Finally, when you are satisfied that you have produced the best letter possible, send it to a native speaker (preferably a fellow academic) and ask them to check it.

PART 2: BAD AND GOOD EXAMPLES (TEMPLATES)

The following letters are designed to highlight the dangers of writing poor emails (BAD EXAMPLES), and the benefits of writing letters with a precise objective (TEMPLATES).

7.9   Erasmus programme

BAD EXAMPLE

Dear Mr. Pohjola,

My name is Diego and I´m a Brazilian Master student of Constitutional Law/Political Science in University of Porto (Portugal).

I was approved for the Erasmus Program in University of Helsinki and they required that I wrote to you, introducing myself and in order to make all the right academic choices.

I´m not sure whether it´s you I ask about documents I need to send via University of Porto.

Anyways, about the core of my studies, since I will be on my thesis year, I got advised to enroll in one class and ask for a co-guide on the thesis, along with the portuguese one (which is yet to be appointed by the University of Porto). Is that possible? How will I be evaluated on the class and by my co-guide? Do you have a list of classes I could choose? Are all of them taught in finnish?

Thank you very much in advance and I´m sorry if I seem a bit lost, I´m at the very beginning of the procedure.

Diego

Diego has written a very friendly letter, and Prof Pohjola (from the University of Helsinki) will probably have a positive impression of Diego's personality. However, the letter is rather too informal - generally speaking, and especially with people whose culture you are not familiar with (e.g. Finland), you should opt to be more formal than you might normally be.

Specific points:

* Use the recipient's academic position (e.g. *Professor, Dr.*) and not *Mr, Mrs* etc.
* *Master student* is not correct: You can say *Master's student* or *I am currently doing a Master's in* + name of subject, or *I have a Master's in* + name of subject

- Many of the prepositions are wrong (see the template version below)
- Avoid mentioning your name at the beginning, simply state i) what kind of student you are (PhD, Master's etc), ii) what and where you are studying.
- Check your spelling and punctuation (*Portuguese* and *Finnish* should have an initial capital letter)
- Delete any phrases that add no value for the reader

TEMPLATE

The parts to change are in italics. Parts in square brackets are optional.

Dear Professor *Name*

I´m a *Master's / undergraduate* student in *subject* at the University of *Town* (*Country*).

I have been approved for the Erasmus Program at *recipient's university*.

I was wondering whether you could tell me what documents I need to send via my university.

I will be in my thesis year, so I have been advised to enroll in one class and ask for a co-tutor for my thesis (I also have a tutor at *applicant's university*). Would that be possible?

[I also have a few other questions:

- How will I be assessed throughout the course?
- Do you have a list of classes I could choose?
- Are all of them taught in *language of host university*?]

[If you are not the right person to ask, please could you kindly forward this email to the relevant person.]

Thank you very much in advance.

First name + last name

7.10   Workshop

Dear Madam/Sir,

my name is Anong Challcharoenwattana, and I am a PhD student in Agroecology at Aarhus University.

With this letter I hereby would like to state my motivation to attend the workshop on agro-ecology and ecological intensification for a sustainable food future, which will be held at the Joint Research Centre (JRC) in Avignon on 13/14 July.

I am writing a thesis about the management of functional biodiversity in low input agriculture. I am investigating how to enhance cover crops potential to suppress weeds and improve soil fertility. My research interests are strictly connected to agroecosystem services, and the ways in which they are provided to society by agriculture. The topic of the workshop is key to my research activity and professional objectives. Therefore, I would highly appreciate to be given the opportunity to attend this event gathering towering scientists and representatives from the EU institutions.

I also perceive this as a possibility to familiarize with good practices, which are essential to my career and personal growth. I firmly believe in the necessity to connect academia with the stakeholders involved in agriculture. Research should strive to provide policy-makers with concrete solutions to environmental issues. I am sincerely convinced that scientific research should meet the fundamental interests of society.

I am confident you will find my application to be a worthwhile investment. I am sure that the attendance at this workshop will be an outstanding opportunity to me, and will pay off for years to come.

Anong has written a competent letter, but the final two paragraphs sound like they were pasted from a website called "How to write an application to go to a workshop" - they don't sound real and could have been written by anyone. When you write any kind of letter ask yourself "what value will the reader gain by reading this sentence / paragraph?"

Specific points:

- ensure you have a heading. This means that the second paragraph in Anong's letter could be reduced considerably (see template version below)
- if you are not addressing your letter to anyone in particular, you can avoid using a salutation

- always begin each paragraph with a capital letter, even the first paragraph after the salutation
- consider using bullets to list your skills, reasons etc
- delete anything that is not specifically aimed at getting your request accepted
- do not write any strange sentences particularly those whose meaning you are not sure of (e.g. *gathering towering scientists, I hereby state my motivation, pay off for years to come*)

TEMPLATE

The parts to change are in italics. Parts in square brackets are optional.

Workshop on psycholinguistics and statistical tools - Atlantis 13/14 July.

I am a PhD student in *psycholinguistics* at *Melbourne University* and I would very much like to attend your workshop.

I am writing a thesis about how *a researcher's name can influence the research field that they choose*. This project has *involved compiling lists of surnames such as Wood, Bugg, Gold and Wordsworth in order to understand the incidence of such names in the fields of forestry, entomology, economics and linguistics, respectively*. To carry out this research *I am using an innovative statistical tool, developed by me and some fellow PhD students, called SirName*.

I believe my research area matches the topic of the workshop because:

- x
- y
- z

[In addition, I think I could share my knowledge in:

- x
- y
- z]

These three points are *at the cutting edge of research in this area, and* fortunately I am working in a top laboratory [name of lab] where I have acquired skills in .... In fact, I believe participants may be interested in learning new techniques about ...

I look forward to hearing from you.

7.11 Summer school

BAD EXAMPLE

I'm very *interesting* in your school because I think it would be *a very useful* for my PhD activity as well very *formative* for my personality.

I'm *apassionate* in neuroscience and I'd like to learn much more about the techniques *sued* in this field.

The main topic of my research *are* neuroengineering techniques, in particular imaging analysis both in-vitro and in-vivo and neuronal models. My research activity is focused on understanding the neural basis of some brain disord*er* such as autism so I'm *specially interesting* in your activity concerning neuropsychological diseases.

I'm at the beginning of my PhD so I have a lot to learn and I think your school would be a wonderful occasion both to have a deeper theoretical background and to get involved in your *laboratories activity*. I'd like to participate *at* two different projects one concerning an fMRI experiments and *one a* microscopic technique so that I can *make practice* in both areas of my research.

Finally I think that attending your school will be a good *occasion* to know the *wroks* of other students and researchers, to exchange opinions and so to increase my knowledge and my experience in the neuroscience field.

The content and structure of the above letter are fine. The problem is the English (see words in italics). The letter contains at least 10 basic mistakes in the use of English, including typos. The issue here is that the candidate clearly didn't take the time to check the letter, and if she didn't check the letter, then by implication she may not be a conscientious person, and thus may not be suitable for the workshop.

TEMPLATE

I would like to apply for a place at your summer school.

I am particularly interested in attending because

- x
- y
- z

I'm passionate about neurosciences and I'd like to learn much more about the techniques used in this field.

The main topic of my research is neuroengineering techniques, in particular imaging analysis both in-vitro and in-vivo and neuronal models. My research focuses on understanding the neural basis of some brain disorders *[link to personal webpage where the candidate's research is outline in detail],* such as autism, so I'm especially interested in your courses on neuropsychological diseases.

I'm at the beginning of my PhD so I have a lot to learn. I think your school would be a wonderful opportunity both to have a deeper theoretical background and to get involved in the activities at your laboratories. If possible, I would like to participate in two different projects: fMRI experiments and microscopic techniques. This would thus enable me to gain experience in both areas of my research.

Finally, I think that attending your school would be perfect for learning about the work of other students and researchers, to exchange opinions, and thus to increase my knowledge and my experience in neurosciences.

I look forward to hearing from you.

7.12   PhD application

BAD EXAMPLE

Dear Prof.,

My name is Miluše Adamik, final year student of Master's in Innovation Management, at the České vysoké učení technické in Prague (Czech Republic).

Currently I am writing my thesis about "network diffusion model of Innovation". My background is industrial engineering. I was visiting the webpage of Innovation Management at UCCIL, and I found a very interesting field of research in Innovation management. I would like to ask for further information about doing a PhD in your institute.

I really appreciate your reply in advance,

Best regards,

Miluše Adamik

Miluše's email looks as if it took 30 seconds to write. Little or no thought has gone into what information the professor might need.

She was lucky to receive the following reply from the professor.

Dear Mr. Miluse, Thank you very much for your interest in our research. Could you please send me your CV? I also some need information about your current Master's studies. Is it a university? What is your current status in the program (grade average)? How long will it take you to finish your studies?

The professor's reply highlights the following:

1. don't write the name of your university or institute in your own language - how can your reader be expected to know what it means (in this case the Czech Technical University)
2. provide clear information about what you are studying now, what types of courses you are following, and when you will finish
3. attach your CV, or provide a link to your CV
4. specify which PhD you are interested in
5. make it clear what sex you are (male or female) - this avoids the recipient replying with the wrong title (*Miluše* = female first name, the professor probably read *Adamik* and thought it was a male first name). The simplest solution is to have a photo in your CV. Alternatively sign yourself, for example, *Miluše Adamik (Ms)* or *Andrea Paci (Mr)*

Miluše's email has other problems, highlighting that you should:

- never address the recipient simply as *Prof*, use the full form (*Professor*) and add their last name (e.g. *Dear Professor Wallwork*)
- avoid repetition
- structure your mail clearly
- think from the reader's point of view and include all the information they may need

TEMPLATE

The parts to change are in italics. Parts in square brackets are optional.

Dear Dr. Wood,

I would like to apply for the PhD project *"Physiological tolerance of tropical forest invertebrates to microclimate change"*.

I am currently doing a *Master's in ecology* at the *University of Zurich*, and I would like to find a PhD program for the next academic year. Last semester I studied *the physiological tolerance of different species of trees to changes in temperature and precipitation*. I would be very interested in *seeing whether as with trees, different species of ants and beetles have different ranges of tolerance to microclimate change*.

I would appreciate if you could take a look at my CV to see if my profile corresponds to the type of candidate you are looking for. If it does, could you please let me know how to apply for the PhD.

Best regards

7.13   Placement

A *placement* and an *internship* in the field of academia are essentially the same thing - a period away from your own institute spent in the team of another research group (generally in another country). However the two terms do have slightly different meanings if the period is spent in industry rather than an academic institution. To learn more: https://www.wikijob.co.uk/wiki/internships-placement-or-internship

Below is an example of a letter where the candidate has been recommended by his/her professor to write to another professor to ask about the possibility of a placement.

GOOD EXAMPLE

Dear Professor Weber

Urma Schmidt was in touch with me recently concerning the possibility of a placement which is a requirement for my Master's in Sociology at Malmö University.

I am required, as part of my course, to find a placement with a research group in Sociology for a minimum period of 39 days from February next year. This can be unpaid work.

I have an interest in social morphology as I worked with Dr Schmidt when she ran the Geographical Data and Settings Laboratory at the RQW. I also have considerable experience in statistics and experimental design.

Dr Schmidt is no longer active in this area but recommended that I apply to you for a potential placement. She informs me that your group is working in many of the areas where I think my experiences might be useful for your team.

I would be very grateful if you would consider me for a placement position within the research group for the period identified, or longer if required by the research project.

I aim to finish my Master's in Sociology and gain skills that will allow me to progress to a Doctoral level. I would like to develop a career in social morphology, and any assistance in gaining the required skills in this area would be greatly appreciated.

Yours sincerely

7.14   Research position / Internship

Dear Professor,

I am S.A. RAMASAMY, I finished my Post-Graduation degree in Computer Science [MCA] from the Indian Institute of Technology. I am keen on doing the research work in Mobile/ Wireless, Computer Networks, Software Engineering, Graphics, Computer Architecture, Operating Systems, Databases & Data Streaming, Internet and Web Technologies. I am a dedicated, innovative team player with a strong academic background in C, C++, Java, Oracle, SQL, Informatica tools, Assembling, Installation, Trouble shooting and Maintenance. I had a work experience in networking field from June 20__ to Sep 20__ and three months of training as a Data warehouse Trainee in Business Intelligence & Solutions, Delhi from Nov 20__ to Jan 20__, and i completed in OCA certificate in Oracle.

So I am applying to the research position to your University. For your kind review, I have attached my curriculum vitae. I assure you that the information said in my vitae is true. So have an eye on my vitae and am expecting a positive reply from you at the earliest. Thanking You

There is nothing in the above email to suggest that it has not been spammed to hundreds of professors. Not a single mention is made of anything specific about the professor's university, department or field of interest. Additional problems:

- your country may have very specific ways of writing your name (e.g. S.A. RAMASAMY) - such ways are fine when you use them within your own country, but not on an international level where the standard is given name + family name
- your cover letter should not contain long lists of technical skills and work experiences, these should be reserved for your CV. Instead you should choose one or two skills or experiences and clearly highlight how these would benefit the institute where you hope to conduct your research
- you should not make subjective statements such as *I am a dedicated, innovative team player* without giving a clear examples that illustrate that you have such skills (see Chapter 9 in *CVs, Resumes and LinkedIn: A Guide to Professional English*).
- avoid any strange statements (*I assure you that the information said in my vitae is true*)
- avoid literal translations from your own language (*So have an eye on my vitae / Am expecting a positive reply from you at the earliest. / Thanking You*) instead use standard English phrases. Note that particularly with regard to written correspondence, Indian English differs from standard British or US English.
- *you* does not require an initial capital letter

TEMPLATE

The example on the next page comes directly from Section 12.35 of Chapter 12 in *Cover Letters in CVs, Resumes and LinkedIn: A Guide to Professional English*. The CV book covers everything you need to know about how to write a CV / resume and write your profile on LinkedIn.

Center for Economic and Policy Research
1611 Connecticut Avenue
NW, Suite 400
Washington, DC 20009

25 November 2028

Full-time Winter International Program Intern January-May 2029

Dear CEPR Staff,

PARAGRAPH 1 I learnt from your newsletter about this interesting opportunity for an intern. In fact, I have read your web pages on a daily basis since I got to know the CEPR from attending Sally Watson's lecture at the *XVIII Encuentro de economistas internacionales sobre problemas de desarrollo y globalización* last March in La Habana, and it has now become an indispensable resource for my understanding of current social and economic problems.

PARAGRAPH 2 I have spent the last academic year at the *Universidad Nacional Autónoma de México (UNAM)* on an Overseas Exchange Student scholarship from the University of Bologna. In the first semester I attended courses of the Maestría en Economía Política and the Maestría en Estudios Latinoamericanos, whereas I spent my second semester doing research for my postgraduate thesis on the perspectives of the regional integration programme *Alternativa Bolivariana para las Américas (ALBA)*.

PARAGRAPH 3 Because of my past experience as head of a cultural association in Bologna I am used to working in a self-directed group and I perform well on both a personal and institutional level. I also have experience in the organization of international events, due to a long collaboration with the University of Groningen in establishing, running and consolidating the European Comenius Course in Bologna.

PARAGRAPH 4 I believe that the combination of my commitment to learning and research-ing, my long standing interest in Latin American issues, the skills gained from past work experience and the knowledge of CEPR commitments acquired in these months of passionate reading, will enable me to contribute immediately and directly to the CEPR as an International Program Intern.

Thank you for your time and consideration,

Best regards

Here is an analysis of the cover / motivation letter on the previous page.

Layout: Everything is aligned to the left, apart from the subject of the letter which is centered and in bold.

Structure: 1) address 2) date 3) subject line 4) opening salutation 5) four paragraphs 6) closing salutation 7) signature 8) reference to the enclosure

Paragraph 1: a) the candidate says where she learned about the position b) she mentions Sally Watson who presumably will be known to the reader c) she shows appreciation for the work that CEPR is doing.

Paragraph 2: Here she shows how what she has studied fits in perfectly with the CEPR's requirements.

Paragraph 3: The candidate states what she can do and then provides strong evidence of it.

Paragraph 4: Again a little pretentious but in reality it makes the candidate sound very sincere, passionate and committed, and in my opinion is a strong ending to her letter.

Below is an example of a longer cover letter / motivational letter.

I would like to apply for a volunteer position for your "New Volunteering @ ToyHouse Project". Please find attached the application form and my CV.

I am 22 years-old, from Pisa (Italy) where I am studying Political Sciences at the University of Pisa. I came to London two years ago, and plan to go back to Italy to finish my degree in June next year.

Currently I'm looking for an opportunity to develop my skills and knowledge in charities and social organizations. The ToyHouse Project appeals to my long-standing interest in childcare and education. In fact, from the age of 15 to 20 I worked as a dance instructor with children from 3 to 12 years of age. It was an amazing working experience that has changed my approach to life and also influenced the choice of my degree. Working with children at such an early age made me really conscious about child labour and how this above all affects developing countries. In addition, during my teenage years I spent I worked at summer camps. My ultimate dream would be to work either in my local community or abroad with NGOs and charities, to help deal with these issues and especially to try to help give these children their childhood back.

I would greatly appreciate the opportunity to be part of your team, and feel sure that your organisation would benefit from my versatile skills. I love spending time with kids and feel that I would be a particularly appropriate person for your Early Years Softplay and Sensory Softplay programs. In addition my fitness training and teaching practice would be appropriate skills for your outdoor Olympic theme program, Hop, Skip & Jump. Furthermore thanks to my experience in the retail sector, I can offer great customer service and help in selecting and stocking toys. Regarding my recent work experience, you will notice from my CV that I have changed jobs quite frequently - each new job has resulted in a higher salary and greater responsibility, and of course, new and useful experiences. I hope you will consider my application because I believe that with my work experience and skills, I would be a positive addition to your team.

I look forward to hearing from you.

Note how the candidate has:

- tried to find the typical things that would be involved in the job and how she would match these needs.
- shown that she is really interested and passionate, and that she has a clear idea of what the job entails. She thus highlights why she is the right person. By doing so she should be able to differentiate herself from all the other applicants.
- mentioned elements from her CV. She has not assumed that the HR person will read her CV in detail
- avoided writing anything that makes it seem that she is exploiting this job opportunity entirely for her own benefit. She makes it look that there will be a clear benefit for her potential employer

Chapter 8

Reference Letters

Factoids

A *U.S. News & World Report* found that 89% of people say rudeness in a work environment is a serious problem, 79% that it's got worse in the last decade, 98% that they themselves are not impolite.

Studies have shown that 95% of US college students are willing to lie to get a job.

Typical excuses for not having done something at work include: *the server was down so I didn't get your mail; my dog ate my consignment; didn't you get my voicemail?*

Fortune magazine once reported that 20-30% of middle managers have written fraudulent internal reports.

The average US worker has 50 interruptions a day, 70% of which have no relation to their work.

A study conducted by Fortune in the 1960s found that teamwork was ranked 10th in the most valued attributes of an employee. A follow up study in the 2000s, revealed that teamwork was in first position.

The three most irritating habits of colleagues in an office environment have been found to be: talking too loud, having an annoying ringtone, talking incessantly on speakerphone.

Working from home has been found to provided more benefits (both for the employee and employer) than working from the office.

If on your office desk you have more than 1 in 5 items that are not strictly work-related (e.g. staplers, pencils) you will be perceived as being unprofessional.

If at various points in the day you do something completely unrelated to your work, you will be more productive when you recommence doing your work.

© Springer International Publishing Switzerland 2016
A. Wallwork, *English for Academic Correspondence*,
English for Academic Research, DOI 10.1007/978-3-319-26435-6_8

8.1 What's the buzz?

Discuss these questions.

- What is a reference?

- Has anyone ever written you a reference? If you managed to see the letter, were you pleased with it? Why (not)?

- When and how should you choose your referees?

- Is it ethical to write your own reference letter and then get your referee to sign it?

****

This short chapter explains:

- what a reference is

- how to get a reference

- how to write a reference

For more details on this topic see Chapter 11 'References and Reference Letters' in *Cover Letters in CVs, Resumes and LinkedIn: A Guide to Professional English.*

8.2 What is a reference?

When applying for an internship or a research position, the candidate is often asked for a 'reference'. A reference is the name of someone (typically a professor) who knows you personally, has tutored you, or whose lab you have worked in.

A 'referee', in the context of job applications, is the person who gives their name as a reference and who may be requested by the 'employer' to give a reference, i.e. a written appraisal of the candidate or an oral appraisal via telephone.

On your CV / resume, it is common to put the names of three or four references, located at the bottom of your CV and laid out as follows:

Professor Ekaterina Alenkina (my thesis tutor), University of London, e.alenkina@londonuni. ac.uk, www.ekaterinaalenkina.com

Professor Johannas Doe (in whose lab I did a 3-month internship), University of Harvard, j.doe@harvard.edu, www.harvard.edu/johannasdoe

Provide the following information:

- name

- their relationship to you

- where they work

- their email address (so that the HR person can contact them)

- their website (so that HR can learn more about them)

8.3 Asking for a reference letter

A reference letter is a letter written by your referee. It covers both you academic achievements and your personality.

The best time to ask for a reference is when you are still in daily contact with your 'referee', i.e. while you are still doing an internship or PhD at the referee's department. You can then ask the referee face to face. This is important as your referee will know exactly who you are, whereas if you wait a few months and contact them by email, they may have only a vague memory of you.

Can you spot any problems with the email below?

Hi Susan,

I am applying for a PhD in Denmark and I was hoping that I could add you as a referee. Here is a link to the PhD offer: http://www.edu.dn/1788674/skole. The deadline is for January 15 so let me know if you are too busy and do not have time to do it. If you don't mind being my referee there is a recommendation form to be filled out before the 15th on this link:

www.edu.dn/1788674/referee.

The code is BORGEN_0608.

Merry Christmas!

Hildegard Bingen

The problems are:

- addressing your ex-professor by their first name may be considered too informal by the recipient (however it may also be appropriate if the professor had an informal relationship with his/her students)

- Susan (the professor who Hildegard wants to act as her referee) may have no memory of who Hildegard is. Remember that professors see hundreds of students every year, and cannot possibly remember who they all are.

In fact, Hildegard received the following email in reply:

> It's been a while since you've been here and I'm rusty on details. To do a reference properly I need an update. Can you send me on an updated CV so I can write a more informed one?
>
> I should be able to find time, but as before please contact me on the 14th just to make sure I don't forget!

In summary:

- remind the referee who you are e.g. *I worked in your lab last summer. I was the student from Germany.*

- provide an up-to-date version of your CV (label the CV with your name)

- put a photo on your CV, so that at least if the referee doesn't remember your name they may remember your face

- give the referee the option not to write the letter (*if you are too busy ...*)

- follow up your email with a reminder nearer the date of your deadline

8.4 Typical questions that a reference letter addresses

The letter typically answers the following questions, which the referee may be asked to answer on an online form provided by the university where you are applying for a position.

1. How long you known the applicant and in what capacity?

2. What do you consider to be the applicant's main strengths and weaknesses?

3. Can you give one or two specific examples of the applicant's performance

4. What is your opinion of the applicant's suitability for an MBA / PhD program?

5. Is there any other information which you feel is relevant?

Alternatively your referee may be contacted directly by the university. Here is a typical mail:

re Ms Haana Mahdad

The above named student has applied to our Department for admission to a Postgraduate Programme of Study (PhD) and has given your name as someone who can inform me of her ability to undertake advanced study and research leading to a higher degree in Physics.

Would you please let me know, in confidence, your opinion of Ms Mahdad's ability, character and capacity for postgraduate study.

Thank you in advance for your cooperation.

If you are applying for a job in a company, then the company might employ an agency to verify that you are who you say are you. These agencies will ask your referee questions such as:

1. When did you last have contact?

2. Having known *name of candidate* for some time, is there anything that you feel we should know that you would consider detrimental to him/her, or about his/her character?

3. Do you have any reason to doubt his/her honesty?

4. If you were looking to fill a vacancy that *name of candidate* had the appropriate experience for, would you employ him/her?

5. How would you sum up *name of candidate*?

8.5   Writing your own reference letter

In order to save your professor time and to ensure that all your achievements and skills are covered satisfactorily, you can write your own reference letter. You then submit it to your professor to sign, making it clear that he/she can modify whatever he/she feels would be appropriate.

To learn how to write a reference letter, see Chapter 11 in *Cover Letters in CVs, Resumes and LinkedIn: A Guide to Professional English.*.

8.6   Structure and template reference letter

The general structure of a reference letter should be similar to the following:

1. Candidate's name in bold, centered

2. Positive opening sentence (*It gives me pleasure to ...*)

3. Referee's position (*I am an assistant professor at ...*)

4. Referee's connection to candidate (*I was the candidate's tutor during ...*)

5. Details about candidate's qualifications

6. Reference to candidate's personality

7. Positive conclusion (*I can strongly recommend the candidate ... I very much hope her candidacy will be taken into serious consideration ...*)

8. Salutation (*Best regards*)

Below is a typical example of a reference letter.

Carina Angbeletchy [1]

I am pleased to have the opportunity to thoroughly recommend Carina Angbeletchy [for the position of ...] [2]

I am a full professor at the Department of Social Sciences at the University of Grenoble. [3]

I was Carina's supervisor while she was doing her Master's of Science in ... She was also a student in my class on linguistic anthropology. [4]

During her Master's thesis, Carina demonstrated great intuitiveness in solving ... In fact, she played a major role in ... She also ... [5]

Although Carina is rather shy and reserved she works extremely well in teams, both as a team member and team leader. She showed a clear demonstration of these skills when ... [6]

I very much hope that her application will be taken into serious consideration as I am sure that Carina Angbeletchy represents an excellent candidate. [7]

Best regards [8]

Chapter 9

Brief Notes on Writing Research Proposals and Research Statements

© Springer International Publishing Switzerland 2016
A. Wallwork, *English for Academic Correspondence*,
English for Academic Research, DOI 10.1007/978-3-319-26435-6_9

9.1   What's the buzz?

1) Imagine you wanted to persuade your university department to provide a course on how to write a PhD proposal. First, think of as many points as possible that you would want to highlight if you were discussing the idea with fellow students. Then select the main points you would want to make if you were trying to convince your department's Board of Advisors.

Think about:

1. What will the board want to know?

2. What is their level of knowledge of the difficulties of writing PhD proposals? How can you inform them better?

3. What other requests for courses (or other activities or equipment) do you think they might get? Why is yours more important?

2) When writing research proposals for funding, researchers typically mention the following points, what else do you think would be crucial to mention?

- Subject / Topic

- Background

- Aims

- Design

- Timeframe

- Cost

****

This chapter does not give full details on how to write a research proposal, but just some key ideas. Further details on how to write in good clear English (but not on the content of a research proposal) as well as how to highlight the importance of your research can be found in Chapters 2-8 of *English for Writing Research Papers*.

This chapter was written with the aid of various experts. Section 9.3 was based on a top professor's advice to a potential PhD candidate. Sections 9.4 and 9.5 take some ideas from the following very useful website: https://chroniclevitae.com/news/820-research-statements-versus-research-proposals. Section 9.5 also draws from a document written by Professor Rolf Norgaard of the University of Colorado at Boulder and entitled *Writing a Statement of Purpose or Research Interest*.

In this chapter you will read some suggestions on how to write:

- a research proposal for external funding

- a research proposal for a PhD program

- a research proposal for a Postdoc position

- a statement of purpose or research interest

9.2   Writing a research proposal for external funding

If you and / or your team are applying for external funding, then you first need to understand who will be evaluating your proposal and how. Below is a quick summary of how reviewers in all parts of the world are likely to conduct their reviews (obviously not all will follow the same five stages, or the same order).

STAGE 1 Reviewers are given up to 15 proposals.

STAGE 2 These reviewers quickly eliminate as many proposals as they can while browsing through them - they don't like wasting their time (similar to how recruiters read CVs).

STAGE 3 They then generally opt for those proposals that are clearly laid out, with clear aims and clear benefits.

STAGE 4 They select four or five proposals to look at in detail.

STAGE 5 Finally they will choose one or two proposals to defend/support/promote at the review meeting. They may try to find fault with the other proposals in order to push forward the ones they have chosen themselves.

So your main aim is to minimize the reviewer's time and effort in reading your proposal. How? Firstly by having clear and realistic aims, and secondly by writing in clear succinct English, which also highlights the novelty of the research.

The kinds of questions reviewers will be asking themselves are:

1. How does the proposed research fit in to to state of the art, and what does it add? Is it original, innovative and groundbreaking?

2. Is it really a problem that needs solving?

3. How multidisciplinary is it?

4. How clear are the objectives? (If the reviewers can't understand your aims they will stop reading your proposal).

5. How feasible and credible are the objectives?

6. How appropriate is the methodology / approach?

7. Do the institutes potentially involved have the right level of expertise?

8. Is the biography of the author of the proposal good and clear?

9. How clearly have the possible results been presented / highlighted?

10. How can these results be exploited in other fields?

11. How realistic are the milestones?

12. How realistic is the cost?

13. Would the potential results justify such a cost?

14. How will industry benefit from the new knowledge acquired?

15. How will it benefit the country / region as a whole? How will it make the country / region more competitive and prestigious?

Essentially you need to 'sell' your idea. Your proposal must not sound dry. Remember that reviewers are going to be choosing between your project and several others (which may be hotter topics than yours). Think about your friends and family - would they be happy to spend their tax money on funding a project like yours? What will happen if your project is not funded? i.e. why does it deserve to be funded? What lessons can be learned from the project that could subsequently be used elsewhere?

See the quote from Professor Norgaard in 9.5 to learn what else you might wish to consider in your proposal.

9.3   Writing a research proposal for PhD or Postdoc position

A research proposal is a document outlining what work you wish to complete during a fellowship period, and how you propose to carry it out.

Below are some suggestions and questions to think about when formulating your research proposal, both for a PhD and for a Postdoc position (see 9.4 for more about Postdoc proposals).

You need to start thinking about your proposal many months before the possible start of the program.

Check whether the institute where you would like to undertake your research has any guidelines that you can follow.

- First of all, focus on your research questions - do they produce new insights or instead do they cover material that has been known for several years and is the subject of many published papers?

- Reflect on what makes you excited about your field of interest, and then think about where you could make a difference. This entails cooperating with your PhD adviser as well as an in-depth study of the literature

- When you have identified an area that you feel passionate about (remember you are going to be spending the next three years on this topic, so you do need to be excited about it!), identify the research gap. What is the problem with the current state of the art? Is this gap something that you can cover in your thesis, i.e. is there enough theory involved? If so, what issues do you have with current theories? How can you advance on them?

- If the problem is related to the technologies currently used, how feasible is it for you to think of a new technology, instrument or method to improve on the state of the art?

- What model (theoretical or real) can you use to test your hypotheses?

Make sure that everything you write will make sense to the reviewer of your proposal. This is particularly the case if you are talking about your own country in relation to the country where your reviewer is located. What may be common knowledge for you, may be alien to the reviewer.

Check that all your sources and literature references are correct.

Finally, note that some of the questions in 9.2 are also worth thinking about when formulating your proposal.

9.4 Differences between a research proposal for a PhD program or Postdoc position

When you are applying for a fellowship for a postdoc position, you need to consider some additional aspects.

You will need to

1. describe your PhD thesis / dissertation, and papers that you have published, and justify why you need to continue studying in this area - you need to be very convincing and compelling

2. outline a timeline of what work you will complete and when (each semester, and each month of the semester)

3. explain what teaching (in relation to your specific research) you might be involved in - describe the course and how you plan to teach it

4. convince your host institution that they will benefit by having you work with them, and that your contribution will advance their mission

Remember that only a very limited number of grants / fellowships will be available. Your proposal must demonstrate that you in particular have the necessary skills, experience and character to achieve the objectives that you have set yourself within a specific time limit.

9.5 Writing a Statement of Purpose or Research Interest

According to Dr Karen Kelsky, author of *The Professor Is In: The Essential Guide to Turning your Ph.D into a Job:*

> A research statement for a job is typically a two-to-four page document that describes scholarship already accomplished, its contribution to a field or fields, and any publications and talks deriving from the research. The statement also describes your next planned project, and the grants, talks, or publications already under way or out related to it.

A statement of purpose or statement of research interest is also often required for graduate school applications, as well as grant and fellowship applications. The purpose of this statement is to give the admissions committee or granting agency a sense of your research interests and/or research agenda. Your statement will also serve as an example of your writing skills.

Given that a research statement is both a summary of your previous research as well as a proposal for future research, it should include both your current aims and findings plus your future goals.

Professor Rolf Norgaard, of the University of Colorado at Boulder, explains:

> As you talk about specific research interests and experiences, be sure to place them in the context of a larger argument about your suitability for graduate work or the value and likely success of your grant project. Be aware that scientists outside of your immediate field or subfield will likely read your statement, so your statement needs to be persuasive to both the narrow specialist and scientists in fields somewhat removed from your own.
>
> It is important, within reason, to customize your statement of purpose or statement of research interest to the particular institution or to the specifications of the grant agency RFP (request for proposals). Avoid sweeping generalizations, clichéd statements, or pie-in-the-sky idealism; you can do so by grounding your assertions through concrete evidence and examples that show you are ready for your next immediate steps as a young professional.

Statements of purpose or research interest are relatively short, typically 500–1000 words. You should consult with the institute where you plan to undertake the research to find out what their selection criteria or rating systems are. This will help you to decide what is important to include, and what you can omit (given the word limit).

Professor Norgaard recommends the following structure:

- first paragraph: short, focus on your goals as they relate to the graduate school or a fellowship or grant; adopt a professional tone

- central paragraphs: make a compelling case that your goals are well-founded and that your career trajectory, as evidenced through particular experiences and personal characteristics, is a good fit with the particular graduate institution or with the specific grant or fellowship

- final paragraph: short; reaffirm your commitment to and preparation for your professional goals

Chapter 10

How to Criticize Constructively

What the experts say

Tact is the art of making a point without making an enemy.

Isaac Newton, English physicist, mathematician, and astronomer

We have "bugs" in the way we think - fundamental errors in how we process information, make decisions, and evaluate situations. ... We tend to ascribe other people's behaviour to their personality, instead of looking at the situation and the context in which their behavior occurs.

Andrew Hunt, 'Pragmatic Thinking and Learning'

Because email is instant it gives us the illusion that we are actually close to our recipient, as if we are actually having a face-to-face conversation. At the same time because we are not actually face to face we feel protected by the anonymity of email, and thus feel more free to make criticisms than we would be if were in front of the person. In an email exchange with a person we don't know very well, we tend to interpret ambiguous phrases in a negative light, making "sinister attributions" that might be unwarranted. Without the second-by-second feedback of a telephone or video exchange, in an email we may continue in a chain of increasingly rude emails.

Janice Nadler, Professor of Law, Northwestern University and Research Professor, American Bar Foundation

© Springer International Publishing Switzerland 2016   123
A. Wallwork, *English for Academic Correspondence*,
English for Academic Research, DOI 10.1007/978-3-319-26435-6_10

10.1 What's the buzz?

1) Choose a paper that you have already written or are currently writing. Exchange your Abstract or Discussion with a colleague. Write a short commentary in note form on what your colleague has written, as if you were a reviewer. When you have finished your notes, discuss with your colleague the difficulties involved in criticizing another person's work.

****

This chapter outlines how to write an informal but critical assessment of a colleague's work.

Writing a review for someone you know is tricky. You certainly don't want to offend them in any way, but at the same time if you find problems in their manuscript, it is clearly beneficial for them to know what these problems are and also how to remedy them. In effect you are acting as a referee, and the more issues you spot now, the more likely the paper will be published on first submission.

10.2 Decide whether email is the best format to make a criticism

Studies conducted by Michael W Morris, professor of Organizational Behavior at Stanford's Graduate School of Business revealed that:

- email is most effective when you already know your recipient

- if you don't know the recipient phone him/her first - such icebreaking can have a very positive impact on the ensuing communication

- if you don't want to call the person, exchange a few pre-emails first before 'getting down to business'

- don't use email for sensitive or awkward topics - you can't 'see' how your recipient will react, and so you can't do any 'damage control'

However, it is unwise to contact your editor by telephone, as the normal procedure is that all communication about manuscripts is conducted via email. In other cases, such as communication with a fellow author, a colleague or with a professor, the telephone might be a better solution if there is any chance of an email message being misinterpreted.

10.3 Think about the context that your reader will be in when reading your email

Before, during or after writing an email ask yourself: What is my recipient's most likely response to my email. Be empathetic. Try to imagine that you are the reader - will you happy, angry, disappointed, disinterested?

Also think about the context that they will be reading your email in. Will they be relaxed and at home, stressed and in the office?

Will your reader think:

- Why should I do that?

- Why has he / she said that? What gives him/her the right to say that?

- Why is he/she telling me this? What do I care?

Try and write from the reader's perspective, imagine their concerns and expectations.

Always avoid being negative. Remember that your recipient is only trying to do his/her best, so being impolite or over-critical is not going to help.

10.4 Structure your email so that the focus is not only on the criticism

A typical situation in the world of academia is when you have to criticize the work, for example, of a fellow colleague, you need to structure your email so that your colleague will react positively despite being criticized.

When someone asks you to have a look at or edit their draft manuscript, they are sharing something with you that may have taken them many months to prepare and which they are probably very sensitive about. Your main aim is to maintain a positive relationship with the person who has asked you to review their work.

Below is a possible eight-part structure.

1) Begin by showing appreciation. Try to create a bridge between you and the recipient in which you show that you want to be helpful and cooperative.

Thank you for sending me the revised version of our paper …

I really appreciate being given the chance to …

It's good to know that you have solved the issues raised by the referees

Thanks for sending me your manuscript. It's looking really good, well done!

I enjoyed reading your paper. It contains a lot of really useful data. I am impressed!

In some way your opening statement should provide 'good news' for your recipient.

2) Demonstrate that you are in agreement of the overall aim of what your colleague is trying to achieve. Show interest in the paper and find areas of the research / manuscript that you are in agreement with.

Your aims seem well grounded and I think there is real innovation.

I think you have highlighted your contribution clearly.

I agree that it is extremely important that we …

You are absolutely right when you say the focus should be …

3) Indicate the parts that you like in what your colleague has done

Your methods are really clear and I think readers would have no problem replicating them.

The abstract looks great. Very clear and concise, and not too much introductory stuff.

Your rewritten Conclusions are much clearer now.

The aims of the paper seem so much more focused now.

4) Identify your concerns (this is the part where you introduce your criticisms)

I notice that …

I am not completely convinced by …

It seems to me that it might be better if we …

Please could you clarify for me why you have …

Make suggestions / Offer to help

5) Tell the authors what you have done.

I have read the manuscript carefully and made several changes to the text, including a couple of additions. I hope that in doing so I have not altered the sense of what you wanted to say. In any case, please feel free to disregard.... Where possible, I have tried to... Nevertheless, I think, the paper still needs some work before you send it to the journal.

6) Make any suggestions in a soft way.
In the past, I have found it useful to ...

The referees might appreciate it if we ...

I think we're nearly there, we just need to ...

I would be very happy to talk through these ideas ...

Let me know if you'd like to Skype some time this week.

7) Offer further help and tell them when you would be available.

If you need any more help, then don't hesitate to contact me. I am on vacation next week, but will be back the week after.

I would be happy to talk through the changes I suggested to the Discussion.

Please keep me up to date with the progress of this manuscript and let me know if you need any further help.

8) End on a positive note
Thanks again for all your hard work on this.

As I said, you've made a substantial improvement to the manuscript. Thank you so much.

10.5   Use the first words set a positive tone

How you write your first sentence will determine how you reader interprets the rest of the email.

If from the the first sentence your recipient perceives your intention as being positive and beneficial, then they will look for such benefits in the rest of the email, i.e. they will selectively look for phrases and evidence that supports this positive first impression. The pattern is similar with a negative first impression. If your recipient perceives aggression or friction, then they will look at the rest of the email trying to find confirmation of this negativity.

It is good practice to say something positive in the first few lines, but be careful how you phrase such comments. For example,

I have looked through your presentation and think it's quite good. Just a few comments:

can be interpreted as being a bit negative. The term *quite good* is a little dangerous in English because it can mean anything from "really good" to "sufficient but nothing great". This is partly due to the fact that words like *quite* very much depend on the intonation they are given when spoken. But of course in an email this intonation is completely lost.

Imagine how you would feel if you received the comments in the first column below. You would probably feel quite discouraged. The comments in the second column immediately put the recipient in the right frame of mind to receive any criticisms that you might have.

NOT VERY ENCOURAGING	ENCOURAGING
Your presentation is OK.	It's looking really good—I love the way you've used photos.
It looks fine.	Overall it looks excellent and the conclusions are very clear.
I looked at your presentation. Here is a list (non-exhaustive) of things you need to change:	I've now had a chance to go through the presentation and I thought you might like a few suggestions.
You need to improve the following points in your presentation:	It's pretty impressive, well done. Here are just a few comments which you are welcome to ignore.

10.6   Be constructive in your criticism

If you need to be critical of someone's work, your recipient is more likely to act on your comments if they are presented in a positive way.

Let's imagine that a co-author has written the first draft of the Methods section of a manuscript describing some research you have done together. Your respective professors set up the collaboration and in fact you don't know this co-author particularly well; he comes from another institute in another country. Most of your communication has been conducted via email and you have only met face-to-face twice.

In your opinion your co-author has committed three crucial mistakes. He has

- missed out some important steps

- not put the sources of some of the materials

- misspelled the names of some of the materials

Here is a typical example of an email that fails to address these points in a constructive way:

Dear Paul

I have had a look at the Methods section and there are several problems with it. First you have missed out two crucial steps (i.e., blah and blah). Second, you haven't spelled some of the names of the materials correctly. Last but not least, you have failed to provide the sources of some of the materials.

I am reattaching the draft with various other suggested changes and additions.

Please could you make the other necessary changes and send me the draft back by the end of this week. It is now quite urgent.

Best regards

Maria

Maria has not thought about how Paul might feel when he reads her email. Paul is likely to be very angry and / or very upset. He may have spent months on writing the Methods. In addition, there may be very good reasons for the three apparent errors. Perhaps the two crucial steps were originally in the manuscript, but Paul had decided to change their position, and had thus cut them out but forgotten to paste them back in (maybe he was interrupted by a phone call when in the middle of the cut and paste). In his email to Maria, perhaps Paul had forgotten to tell her that he was locating the sources of some of the materials and would get back to her with the details. And finally, maybe Paul was waiting for Maria's revisions before doing a final spell check.

Maria's email will have a negative impact because

- it does not give the recipient the benefit of the doubt; it assumes that there is no other explanation for Paul's three errors other than that he is incompetent

- it is very direct; there is no introduction

- it over-emphasizes the problems by using words like *failed* and *last but not least*; it thus seems quite sarcastic

- its tone is not that of a co-author, but that of a severe angry professor

If you begin your email with an immediate criticism, your co-author will react negatively and this will set the tone for how he reacts to your other comments.

Instead find something positive to say. Here are some examples:

> Thanks for getting this section to me far ahead of the deadline; this will make my life much easier.

> I really like your succinct style of writing; I think it will help the referees, and the readers, to follow our methodology easily and quickly.

> Although I am not a native speaker myself, your English seems to be really good—so let's hope the reviewers are impressed!

Provided they are sincere, the above sentences help to get the recipient in a positive state so that he will then read your criticisms with a more open mind. You then have to deal with the three main mistakes in his draft. The first thing is to try and reduce the number of criticisms you make, and then begin with the most serious mistake. Thus, Maria's email could be rewritten as follows:

> I just wanted to point a couple of issues in your draft. Firstly, I may be wrong, but it seems to me that you have missed out two important steps in our methodology. These are …

> Secondly, the editor will expect us to provide the sources for all our materials, so I think we need to add these. I think I only noticed a couple of cases, so this shouldn't take you too long.

> By the way, would you mind doing a final spell check, but not just with Word as I don't think it will identify any spelling mistakes in the technical names (e.g., the names of the source materials).

In her revised version, it seems that she is only making one criticism (the two steps that are missing) and she does this by softening her comments with *I may be wrong, but it seems to me*. This gives Paul the option to prove her wrong. Regarding the sources of the materials, Maria takes joint responsibility for this by using the inclusive pronoun *us* and *our*, and she then minimizes the effort required by referring to the small number of sources involved and the short time required to sort out the problem. Finally, she presents the reference to the spelling mistakes almost as an afterthought (*by the way*) and as a friendly request (*would you mind*).

So, when Paul reads the above message, he will be appreciative of Maria's comments and will be more likely to both implement them and get back to Maria quickly.

10.7 Be diplomatic and make detailed comments rather than unspecific observations

When making your comments, it is generally appropriate not to sound overcritical and harsh but to adopt a more diplomatic, less direct approach. Compare these pairs of sentences and note how those in the second column adopt a softer approach.

DIRECT CRITICISM + TOO GENERIC	INDIRECT CRITICISM + MORE SPECIFIC
You should re-write parts of the presentation.	I think the introduction (i.e. Slides 2-3) may need some re-working.
Cut the redundant slides.	Could we manage without Slides 5 and 6? / It might be an idea to cut Slides 5 and 6
The Methodology is way too long.	What about making some cuts to the Methodology (e.g. the flow chart)?
You'll never have time to explain all those slides on the Results.	If we wanted to make any cuts anywhere, the Results might be a good place to start (e.g. the first two tables). / I understand why you have gone into such detail in the Results, but…

The examples above highlight various important points about softening the tone:

- choice of action words: *rework* is must less dramatic than *rewrite*

- use of modals of obligation (should, must): these are best avoided in active sentences as they tend to sound too authoritarian. If you are using such words simply to express an opinion, then begin your phrase with *I think*, or *it might be a good idea if*, etc.

- *may, might, perhaps, possibly*: these words are excellent ways to make suggestions without appearing to be a know-it-all

- phrasing criticisms in the form of questions: this allows for a certain amount of doubt, whether real or not, on the part of the commentator to be transmitted to the author. It also leaves the decision up to the recipient, thus leaving him / her feeling more in control.

- beginning sentences with *if*: the conditional can always be used as a more indirect means to criticize

- use of *we*: this makes you sound more involved in the process, as if you are sharing the responsibility with the author. This transmits a feeling of collaboration, rather than the idea of me vs you.

- use of words like *understand* and *appreciate*: again these help you sound more understanding, and show that you appreciate all the hard work the author has done

Also, note how the suggestions in the second column are much more specific than the vague comments in the first column.

10.8   Avoid being too direct when asking for clarification and making suggestions

When you are not sure about something that your colleague has written, it's a good idea to be careful how you ask questions and avoid being too direct otherwise you could sound more critical than you intend. You can make a question softer by

1. adding an extra little introductory phrase

2. making out that it's you that has a difficulty, but not necessarily that this difficulty is caused by some negligence on the recipient's part

3. phrasing the question in the passive, thus making it appear that the author was somehow not involved in the decision when in fact they were

DIRECT QUESTION	INDIRECT QUESTION
Why don't you have an "Outline" slide?	By the way, have you thought about having an "Outline" slide?
When are you going to mention the disadvantages of our approach?	Have you decided when you are going to mention the disadvantages of our approach?
Why did you include the table in the fourth slide?	It was probably my idea, but can you remind me why it was decided to include the table in the fourth slide?

Of course, if you have a lot of comments to make or if your comments are simple observations that will clearly help to improve the content of the presentation, then there is no need to always adopt a roundabout approach. For example:

The weight should be quoted to 3 decimal places, not 4.

An easier solution would be to swap the position of slides 5 and 7.

Don't forget to do a spell check at the end (I always forget!)

In the above cases you are not criticizing the recipient but merely making some helpful suggestions.

10.9   When you have some good to say use shorter sentences; use longer sentences for 'bad' news

Short sentences stand out from the text. So phrase your positive reactions to your recipient using shorter sentences. It is claimed that the Wall Street Journal encourages its writers to use nine words a sentence. And Rudolf Flesch advised keeping sentences to 11-14 words. However, when you have to refuse a request, give someone bad news, or say 'no' in general, you might want to use longer sentences. Use the length of the sentence to reduce the drama of the situation.

10.10   Use positive wording

When you have written your email see if you can turn potentially negative sounding words into something positive.

Sorry to have *disturbed* you with this.

= I hope this may have been of *help*

Thank you for you *trouble*.

= Thank you for your *help*.

I *won't* be able to get the paper to you until May 30.

= I *will certainly* be able to get the paper to you by May 30.

10.11   Conclude your report by saying something positive

Your concluding comments should always be positive, thus leaving the recipient thinking that they have not made a complete disaster of their work. Make sure you don't simply end with *Regards, Carlos* but include a phrase like one of the following:

> Thanks for doing such a great job on this, and also thanks for offering to do the presentation (I am sure you will do it much better than I would have done).

> Well, I think that's all—once again, a really excellent job, just a few things to tighten up here and there.

> Hope you find these comments useful, and bear in mind that I've only focused on what changes I believe need making so I'm sorry if it comes across as being very critical.

10.12   Re-read everything before you hit the "send" button

Always re-read what you have written when you have been criticizing someone's work (or whenever you have something potentially awkward to say). Make sure you haven't said anything that could damage your relationship or offend in any way. Also, if you really have to be critical, consider leaving the email for a while and then coming back to it to see if you have been really fair or not.

Before you send the mail, let other colleagues look at it to check it is not aggressive or open to being interpreted as being aggressive. If you are feeling angry, then it pays to save the email and review it again the next day before sending it.

And remember that other people may read your email too. The danger of having something written is that can be used against you, and perhaps out of context.

10.13   Be diplomatic when sending reminders

If you are a PhD student or junior researcher and you make a request (e.g., to review your work), your recipient is generally under no obligation to fulfill the request. So if you hear nothing it is a good idea to send them a reminder (known as "chasing" in English). Ensure that you do so in a friendly tone with no sense of frustration or anger. Here are some examples:

> I was wondering if you had had time to look at my email dated 10 February (see below).

> I know that you are extremely busy, but could you possibly…

Sorry to bother you again, but I urgently need you to answer these questions.

I know you must be very busy but if you could find the time to do this …

When you chase someone with regard to a previous email that you have sent, always include the old email within your new email—this is why in the first example sentence above the sender has put *see below*. This indicates that the old mail is below his / her signature of the new email.

It may help to motivate your recipient to reply if you do one or more of the following:

- empathize with the fact that they are a busy person who probably has more important things to do than to reply to your request

- explain why this person is important for you and your work

- give them a brief explanation as to why you need a reply so urgently

- tell them how long it will take them to fulfill your request—people always tend to overestimate the time of a task that they don't want to do

- if time is running short, reduce your original request to what is absolutely essential for you (e.g., maybe originally you asked someone to read your whole manuscript, now you just ask them to read just one section)

- find a benefit for them of fulfilling your request

- give them a deadline for their response

Here is an example of an email from a student writing to a professor who she has never met for advice on her manuscript.

Dear Professor Li

I was wondering if you had had time to look at my email dated 10 February (see below).

I imagine that you must receive a lot of requests such as mine, but I really need your input as no one else has your expertise in this particular field. In reality, it would be enough if you could just read the last two pages of the Discussion (pages 12 and 13), just so that you could check that I have not reached any erroneous conclusions. I very much hope that my results might be of interest to you too as they diverge from what you reported in your paper *paper title*. I have a deadline for submission on the 20 April, so it would be perfect if you could get your comments to me by about 10 April.

I realize that this is a lot to ask, particularly as you have never even met me, but if you could spare 10-15 minutes of your time, I would be extremely grateful.

I look forward to hearing from you.

10.14 Be appreciative when thanking someone for doing an informal review of your work

When someone has done you the favor of reviewing your manuscript, it pays to be appreciative of their work. This is irrespectively of whether their comments were useful to you or not, and of whether you agree with what they say. You can begin an email of thanks by saying:

> Thank you so much for your review, it was very kind of you to spare the time. The manuscript has certainly benefitted from your input—particularly the Discussion, where you have managed to really highlight the novelty of the research.

If they have made any specific criticisms you can say:

> I understand what you meant by… so I have adjusted that section accordingly.

> Clearly, having read your comments, I need to rewrite the part about…

> I think you were right about the table, so I have…

If you need any clarifications, you can say:

> Thanks very much for all this. Just one thing—could you just clarify exactly what you mean by …

> I may come back to you if I need further thoughts on some of the slides.

Also, bear in mind that if this person has made certain comments, they may be the exact same comments that the referees might make. Thus, it is worth taking your colleague's comments into serious consideration.

You can conclude your email by something like:

> Once again thanks for all your hard work—I found it really useful. I will keep you posted about the progress of the manuscript.

Chapter 11

Writing a Peer Review

What some reviewers say

The paper is ill-informed and poorly argued. It is not suitable in my view for this or any other journal.

I've never read anything like it and I do not mean it as a compliment.

Are you kidding?

I have read this paper several times through, and I have nothing to say in its defense.

You aimed for the bare minimum, and missed!

It is early in the year, but difficult to imagine any paper overtaking this one for lack of imagination, logic, or data—it is beyond redemption.

Was this an undergraduate class assignment?

The writing and data presentation are so bad that I had to leave work and go home early and then spend time wondering what life is about.

This submission looks more like an advertising booklet rather than a research paper.

This result would be great if it were true.

This paper must be rejected, because the work it describes is clearly impossible.

This paper is so bad, it would take an entire 20 page paper to describe all the problems it has. And even after that I'm not sure it would be worth publishing.

© Springer International Publishing Switzerland 2016
A. Wallwork, *English for Academic Correspondence*,
English for Academic Research, DOI 10.1007/978-3-319-26435-6_11

11.1   What's the buzz?

The reviews in the Factoids and many quoted in 11.11 and 11.14 were taken from the following website: http://shitmyreviewerssay.tumblr.com/

This is a great site, and if you are ever the victim of sarcasm then I suggest you submit to it. In addition, if you are reviewer yourself, scroll through the site to ensure that you are not regularly writing abusive or unhelpful reviews.

Discuss the following.

1. Generally speaking, how well do you react to criticism of your work?
2. Does it make a big difference how such criticism is expressed?
3. Have you ever had a paper reviewed?
4. What do you think are the qualities of a good reviewer?

****

Peer review is an essential part of research. If you are chosen to do a peer review, it is because you are considered to have specialized knowledge of the subject. The fact that you were not involved in the research itself enables you to provide an objective and balanced critique of the authors' work. Thus, you are in a perfect position to really help, rather than discourage, the authors in their research, even if it means that you ultimately decide that a manuscript is not suitable for publication.

An analysis of referees' reports by Magda Kouřilová from Comenius University in Bratislava found that less than 10% of her sample reviews used a sandwich technique (i.e., preceded and followed by compliments - see 11.9). Much more common was criticism alone, with no positive comments, even in those papers that were subsequently accepted for publication.

In a paper entitled *How well does a journal's peer review process function? A survey of authors' opinions*, the researchers found that authors awaiting publication disagreed with their reviewers' comments about 25% of the time.

Please note that in this chapter and throughout this section, the terms *referee* and *reviewer*, and *report* and *review*, are used indifferently.

In this chapter you will learn how to:

- follow the recommendations of your journal on how to write a peer review

- focus on constructive feedback rather than negative criticism

- use a "sandwich" approach, in which your criticisms are sandwiched between positive comments

- choose a style and layout that is easy to follow and comment on for the authors

11.2   Be clear about your role as a reviewer

Your main aims as a reviewer are

1. to assess on behalf of the journal whether or not a paper is suitable for publication

2. help a fellow researcher who may be at the beginning of their career and who may not have access to all the data / equipment / experience / funds that you have

11.3   Read your journal's review guidelines

Most journals ask you to review a manuscript by following certain criteria. These criteria are normally contained within a form that you are asked to fill in, or may simply be in a downloadable document containing advice on how to write reviews. In some cases you may be asked to write an informal review for a colleague or a student. Below are some typical aspects that a review is likely to cover, followed by questions that you might like to ask yourself.

The paper should:

CONTRIBUTE TO THE SPECIFIC AREA OF KNOWLEDGE

Does the paper add sufficiently to the current literature? Does the review of the literature display patterns in earlier research that have not been noticed before? What original elements does it add and how? Does it have a clear message? Is the problem well defined and the purpose clearly stated?

HAVE A RELEVANT TITLE

Does the title attract the reader's attention and also reflect the actual content of the paper? Would an intelligent search be able to find this paper?

HAVE AN ABSTRACT THAT IS SHORT YET COMPREHENSIVE

Does the abstract give the reader a good idea of what to expect from the paper? Does the abstract clearly state the main objective (the research question), the conclusions, and how have they been reached, for example, theoretically, by case studies or through other measures?

MAKE GOOD USE OF KEY WORDS

Do the keywords describe the content? Will they enable potential readers to search for and find the paper?

REVIEW EXISTING LITERATURE AND GIVE APPROPRIATE REFERENCES

Have the authors avoided too many references referring to general knowledge or to papers published by the author's co-nationals or just in their own country? Are the references given in the literature cited section at the end of the paper relevant and up to date, have the important ones been included, and are there any important references missing? Are the references mentioned within the body of the paper?

FULLY DESCRIBE THE RESEARCH METHOD

Do the authors make it clear what was done and why certain methods were chosen and others not? Is the study designed well? Does the authors' data set seem appropriate to the questions that they pose? Have appropriate materials been selected? Is the sample of an adequate size? Are the methods adequately described? Can they be easily repeated?

HAVE A DISCUSSION AND CONCLUSIONS

Do their results answer their research question? Are the results well presented, discussed in light of previous evidence, and credible? Could they be strengthened? Are the conclusions justified from the evidence given? Are the conclusions adequately qualified? Are there any logical and obvious possible interpretations that the authors have not mentioned? Have any implications and applications been outlined?

BE CLEARLY ORGANIZED AND WRITTEN

Is the paper laid out clearly, with headings that enable the reader to understand the main points of the paper and to follow its structure? Is the order of the sections, paragraphs, and sentences logical—or should parts be shifted to another location in the paper? Is the style academic, but at the same time reader-oriented, that is, easy to read and assimilate? Is there any redundancy? Could the paper be shortened without losing any value?

HAVE FIGURES AND TABLES THAT ADD REAL VALUE

Do the figures and tables illustrate important points, or are they more confusing than clarifying? Are they explained in the text? Are the captions / legends appropriate?

11.4 How to structure a referee's report: (1) acceptance subject to revisions

A referee's report which recommends possible acceptance subject to changes being made could be structured as follows.

1. SUMMARY OF PAPER

   This helps the authors to see whether you have understood the essence of their paper, and the editor to understand how relevant the paper is to his / her journal.

2. GENERAL COMMENTS ON THE QUALITY OF THE PAPER

   This is a good opportunity to say something positive and encouraging about the paper before beginning to make any criticisms). So, mention the strong points of the paper first, and then the weak points.

3. MAJOR REVISIONS REQUIRED

   Here you suggest what major changes you think the paper needs in order for it to be publishable in the journal. Again, try to present these changes in a constructive way and help the authors to see why such changes are necessary. Number each comment—this helps the authors when responding and the editors in judging the author's response.

4. MINOR REVISIONS REQUIRED

   These generally include typos, changes to numbering, changes to figure legends, suggestions for more appropriate vocabulary, etc. Number each comment.

5. FINAL COMMENTS

   Since your aim is to further knowledge in your field through new research, it helps if you offer some encouraging words of advice and to reiterate the positive elements that you have found in the manuscript. This is particularly important for researchers from less developed nations who may not have the equipment and experience that you have access to, but may nevertheless have discovered something that could benefit people living in their area of the world.

11.5 How to structure a referee's report: (2) complete rejection

If you are recommending that a paper be rejected either because it is outside the scope of the journal or because it would require too many revisions, then you would begin with Points 1 and 2 as in 7.3 above. Even if you are going to recommend rejection, you should still be able to find something positive to say. Points 3 and 4 are not necessary. So finish with Point 5 and if possible make suggestions on what would be required to make the paper more publishable. This will enable the authors to revise their paper and maybe submit it to another (possibly less prestigious) journal.

11.6 How to structure a referee's report: (3) acceptance as is

Even if you are recommending a paper for acceptance with no changes, you still need to provide authors and editors with a brief summary (Point 1 in 7.3). If you think the scientific quality is good, but that the English needs some improvement, then ask yourself how much the "poor" English really impacts on the reader's ability to understand. You can delay a paper's publication unnecessarily by making comments on the English. Of course, if the English is truly bad, then you must let the authors and editor know. See 11.16 and 11.17 for more on this important aspect.

11.7 Bear in mind the authors' expectations of you as a reviewer

I asked a group of 50 PhD students from around the world what they thought were the qualities of a good reviewer. Some of the adjectives they used to describe a good reviewer were as follows:

competent

consistent

constructive

highly knowledgeable

neutral

scrupulous

sympathetic

Below are some of their comments. A good referee should

- understand the difficulties that PhD students have in writing their papers

- write their review in an organized way so that the corrections that need to be made (both in terms of data and the manuscript itself) can be easily followed

- be an expert in the field of reference of the paper and at the same time have no interest in promoting or censoring the papers he / she receives

- indicate how to improve the manuscript so as to make it more readable

- clearly explain the reasons why the paper could not be accepted, without being destructive

- understand what the authors have failed to do correctly and propose "best practices" to correct them based on his / her own experience

- search out errors in the text and clearly explain why they are errors

- have respect for different viewpoints and not be judgmental

- remember that the authors may have spent several years on the research and subsequent writing of the paper and so they should pay it close attention

- the more supportive they are in their comments, the more they will help the author(s)

- be quick to return their reports

11.8   Before you begin your report, put yourself in the author's shoes

It helps to remember the first time you received a referee's report. How did you feel when the referees made non-constructive negative comments? In my job as an editor of research papers, I get to see hundreds of referee reports. Here is one that a young PhD researcher received on her first paper. After reading this report, she was considering abandoning research forever.

The claims made by the author are neither novel nor convincing. The study is of little or no interest to the community, and is probably inaccessible to anyone outside the author's presumably very small research group. Moreover, I believe there are no further experiments that would strengthen the paper.

I found the manuscript painful to read, with no enthusiasm on the part of the authors, nor any regard to a potential application of their work, which would seem to confirm my suspicions that there are no possible applications for this line of research.

The introduction of the work is poorly done with few references to related works. The writing itself is weak—multiple paragraphs are lumped into giant paragraphs without any thought for the poor reader. I struggled to find any connection between one sentence and the next. A literal translation using Google Translate would probably have produced a more merit worthy level of English.

In short, this paper is not worthy of further consideration.

Fortunately, the other two reviewers were kinder, and after some modifications the paper was published in another journal.

11.9 Use the sandwich approach: begin and end on a positive note

Your report should always be constructive in its criticism. Your aim is to help, rather than destroy.

Always begin your report in a positive way. If you do this, the authors will be more prepared to accept the negative things that you have to say. And always end your report positively. Again, this will be appreciated by the authors who at the end of your report will thus not be too disillusioned. Very negative feedback is likely to produce very negative consequences. An author may feel very angry and resentful when their research is torn apart by the reviewer, and may end up actually learning nothing from the experience.

Below is a good example of a general summary of a manuscript. This summary precedes the detailed comments.

The author should be commended for employing data on x in order to analyze y. Although these data present a rich source of information for studying y, they remain largely underutilized, so it is good to see them being used here.

Unfortunately however, the paper, as it is, fails to make an important contribution to the literature, for two reasons. First, the analysis suffers from a number of methodological shortcomings, which are summarized in the "main comments" section below. Second, most of the empirical results are quite obvious.

Having said that, there is one result that seems non-obvious and interesting, namely that … In fact, the paper could be improved significantly if the authors could answer the following questions … If the answer is "yes" to these questions, then these aspects could be further explored. For example, it would be interesting to identify …

In the first paragraph the reviewer shows her appreciation of one aspect of the paper and recognizes the novel value of what the authors have done. In the second paragraph, she outlines the reasons why she will subsequently recommend the paper be rejected subject to major revisions. In the last paragraph she gives the authors some possible avenues to help improve the quality and interest of the manuscript. She does so in a way which shows her obvious enthusiasm for the topic area. The result is that the authors have something positive to work on; they will not end the reviewer's report by thinking "maybe I should try to get a job in industry!"

To help the authors feel more positive about your comments, and thus more likely to implement your recommendations, try not to overuse such nouns as *failure*, *error*, *mistake*, *loss*, *problem*, *inaccuracy*, and *miscalculation*. And completely avoid words such as *disaster* and *catastrophe*. Resist the temptation to be sarcastic or funny at the author's expense; thus avoid adjectives such as *useless*, *hopeless*, *unbelievable*, *absurd*, and *debatable* and expressions such as *the poor reader*.

Make sure that any critical judgments you make are fully supported by detailed reference to the literature. Also, be realistic in the changes that you expect the authors to make. Journal editors always appreciate a positive and constructive approach. It reassures them that they made the right choice in choosing you as a referee.

11.10   Use a soft approach when criticizing

Given that your aim should be to help rather than destroy the author, try to adopt a soft approach. Here are some ways to write comments that are more likely to be accepted and appreciated by the authors.

By avoiding being too direct, the author is more likely to accept, and understand the need for, the negative feedback.

NO	YES
The whole data set seems to say: "OK, X does not change Y." Of course! what were you expecting from a one-year experiment? Why bother putting this in the paper at all?	The authors *might consider* removing this section from the paper as I am not convinced it leads to any worthwhile or conclusive results. Instead, *they could* focus on the interesting part of their work, which is ….

Make your comments sound subjective.

NO	YES
It is absolutely wrong to state that x = y.	*I feel that / As far as I can see, / In my opinion / I believe / Based on my knowledge of the topic I would* say that the assertion that x = y may be *open to discussion.*

If you state that something "must" be done, or that something is "not complete," try to think of how these problems could be remedied.

NO	YES
The presentation of results must be deeply modified.	*I would suggest* that the results be presented in a different way; for example, a table could be used rather than a figure. This *would make* the results stand out better and make it easier for the reader to understand the importance of them.
The description of methods is incomplete and does not permit a correct evaluation of the trials.	The description of the methods needs more details. For example, what criteria were used to select the three byproducts? Why was the field test conducted with KS only? Which parameters did the Authors evaluate in the field test and how?

Try to be helpful and give authors the benefit of the doubt.

NO	YES
The methodological part refers to rather old methods; how can they not be aware of the new procedures existing in the analytical literature?	The authors may not be aware that there are actually some new procedures existing in the analytical literature. They might try reading ....

There are some qualitative words in English that can be interpreted in more than one way (positively, but often negatively). So be careful of how you use words such as *OK* and *quite*.

If you say *The title is OK* it may be interpreted as "just sufficient but nothing special." It might be better to say *The title is fine / very appropriate.*

Similarly, *the results are quite interesting* is ambiguous. It could be they are surprisingly interesting, but more likely the interpretation will be that they really state nothing new.

The end result should be a report that the authors will find useful and which will encourage them to go forward. It should never make them feel angry (even if the paper is going to be rejected) or humiliated.

You will thus be potentially increasing knowledge in a particularly area by encouraging the authors to go back and try again.

11.11   Avoid the temptation to insult the author

Some papers are truly terrible. However your job is to be constructive and to help the researcher improve his / her work. This does not give you permission to offend the author. Statements like the following are unacceptable:

> Why don't you just send copies of this to the two people in the world who care about it, and forget the publication route?

> I want to vomit; I can't believe this paper was submitted.

> The regression analysis is rubbish. Let's see what happens when you do this properly.

> This paper reads like a woman's diary, not like a scientific piece of work.

If you are a native speaker don't use your command of English to belittle the non-native speaker. Also bear in mind that much of your so-called humor will be lost on the non-native researcher, particularly if couched in obscure, arcane or slang expressions such as these:

> I appreciated how the author seemingly had in mind that a goodly percentage of the readership are not native speakers, so anything too academic or erudite might be lost on them.

> It would be charitable to call this a comparison of apples and oranges. It's more like steak and bicycle.

> The authors merely used somewhat bigger guns than previous studies and generated nothing but more smoke.

> A blizzard of extraneous data external information should be culled.

148

Once I penetrated the pigeon English, I found very little substance underneath.

The conclusion is something of a shaggy dog.

This kind of prose simply borders on cruelty against the reader. And finally comes the conclusion, which is the intellectual equivalent of bubblegum.

Find your inner nerd—it must be a big part of you—and then dump it in the ocean tied to a large rock.

Note: All the above were taken from http://shitmyreviewerssay.tumblr.com/

11.12   Don't just use *should* to make recommendations

When you make recommendations, it is best not to be too strong or too direct, otherwise you may give the impression of being rather authoritarian. Using *must* and *have to* is generally not appropriate (e.g., *the authors must reduce the length of the manuscript*); it is better to use *should*. But to avoid repetition and tedium, you cannot use *should* every time you make a recommendation. Consider using the following alternatives:

The authors should explain X.

Please could you explain X.

I would recommend / suggest that the authors explain X.

It would be advisable to explain X.

It might help the reader if the authors explained X.

Also, in the cases above, you should make it clear why the authors need to explain X. If you don't provide the authors with a motivation, then they may not understand the necessity of explaining X. For example:

Given that an understanding of X is crucial in order to appreciate the quality of the results, I suggest that …

I am not sure that readers will be able to follow the experimental procedure if they don't first have a clear understanding of X.

11.13   Use separate paragraphs to outline your comments

Try to make it as easy as possible for both the editor and the author to read your comments. If you write everything in one long paragraph, it will make it very hard for the authors to respond to what you have asked them to do.

Divide your comments into sections with headings—these are normally indicated by the journal.

Have separate paragraphs for each point you make. Give clear page and line references to show where your comments refer to in the paper.

If possible, number each comment.

11.14   Make sure your comments are explicit and explain how they could be implemented

Whether you are recommending acceptance or rejection, all the points you make should be clear to the authors.

The following unhelpful comment is quite typical of a referee's report. It makes a criticism, without suggesting any remedies:

> One of my main concerns is that the level of pollution in the sediments has not been clearly characterized: on the basis of metal contents in sediments (Table 1) it is hard to establish a level of pollution; consequently, the validation of the methodology is quite weak.

A more helpful report would be:

> I have three main concerns:
>
> (1) the aim of the work is not clear—I am not completely sure whether this is simply a validation of a widely-used bioassay or a field study. If it is indeed a validation, then I am not sure of its utility, given that many cases have already been reported in the literature (as cited by the authors themselves). If it is a field study, then it might be useful to add more parameters.
>
> (2) the parameters that the authors measured are too similar to each other and there are too few of them (only four). I would recommend using at least six parameters.

(3) the sediments that the authors chose are not very revealing in terms of metal pollution. What about using sediments from .... ?

The revised version tells the authors what they can do to improve their work (see the last sentence in each of Points 1–3).

In the next example it is not 100% clear which part of the referee's sentence the author needs to address:

Can the authors explain why the artificial seawater for the control was replaced daily?

Is the problem with *artificial* seawater (rather than real seawater), with the *control* (rather than the sample), or with the replacement being on a *daily* basis (rather than hourly or weekly)? A clearer question would be:

Why didn't the authors treat the control in the same way as the other samples (which did not undergo daily replacement)?

In the following sentence the referee gives no reason for the "contrast" or why the sentence is not "clear"; therefore, the authors have little information on which to base the requested revision.

Lines 40–42: this sentence seems to be in contrast with the "Conclusion" section. Please clarify.

Line 51: ...sediments represent the major repository of integration and accumulation of... This sentence is not clear.

The referee is forcing the authors to make an interpretation, which may or may not be correct. The above two comments could be made more explicit by saying:

In the Abstract (lines 40–42) the authors say that x and y were effective, but in the Conclusions it seems that only x is effective.

I am not sure how a repository can contain "integration." What exactly do the authors mean by "integration" in this context?

Always identify which part of a sentence you don't understand and why it is not clear for you.

Here are some more examples of unhelpful comments because they give no explanations.

The length of the paper could be reduced considerably.

The Discussion is rather poor.

The Conclusions do not add to the overall scientific knowledge in the field.

The format of the tables is inadequate.

The simulation analysis is not convincing.

In each of the above examples, the authors will want to know why the reviewer has made such comments and what they can do to remedy them. For example, how could they reduce the length—by cutting certain sections? by removing figures and tables? by reducing the literature cited? by reducing redundant words and phrases?

11.15   Use *you* to address the authors, and *I* (i.e., the first person) to make reference to yourself

Traditionally, referees address the authors as "the authors." Given that the referees' reports are above all for the authors, a much more direct and simpler way to refer to the authors is to say "you." This also avoids ambiguity if there are any third-party authors involved, for example, when the referee needs to talk about the authors of other papers in the literature.

A lot of trouble is taken to see that referees remain anonymous. However, this does not mean that if you are a referee you have to refer to yourself in a very indirect way. The first phrase below, to me at least, sounds very unnatural, and could easily be replaced with the second without any loss of anonymity:

Specifically, this referee is concerned with the following issues …

Specifically, I am concerned with the following issues …

The unnaturalness of not using the first person pronoun (I) is also revealed in the following example:

However, *in the reviewer's opinion*, several critical weaknesses (enumerated below) affect the strength of the paper, which *it is believed* should not be accepted for publication.

It is believed presumably means *I believe*.

11.16   Don't make indiscriminate comments about the level of English

Here are some typical comments made about the level of English of the authors, the first by a non-native speaker of English, the second by a native speaker.

A big problem with this work is the English form: there are so many language errors that it actually seriously compromises one's ability to understand what is being presented. The paper needs an extensive revision by a native English speaker.

While I sympathize with the difficulties of writing in a foreign language, the poor quality of the English was asking too much of me. In the end I gave up. I also found their method of grand-standing their results to be quite obnoxious at times.

It is important to bear in mind that

- the authors' level of English may be quite low, so your report should be expressed in very simple English

- funds may be a problem for them, so anything you can do to prevent them from having to spend extra money and to increase their chances of being published will be helpful

- they may be quite young, so you don't want to discourage them

If you are unsure about the level of English of the authors, it is advisable NOT just to say that the "the paper needs some revision". The problem is that you may unnecessarily:

- force the authors to spend money on a professional proofreader—it is possible that the editor of the journal too may not be a mother tongue English speaker and may not be very well qualified to judge the level of English

- delay the publication of the paper

In any case, do not be vague when criticizing the English.

If you are certain that there are lots of mistakes, you can say:

This paper needs a thorough revision by a native English proofreader.

If there are only some typing / spelling mistakes:

There are a few typos that need correcting (I suggest the authors turn on the spell check in Word)

If there are just a few grammatical mistakes:

I noticed the following grammatical mistakes [*give a list*] but otherwise the English seems fine.

If you are certain there are some mistakes, but you are not sure how to identify them:

> I don't feel qualified to judge the English, as it is not my mother tongue; however, I do feel that in some parts the English is not up to standard and is sometimes rather ambiguous.

If you think the English is good, but you can't be certain, then the simplest solution is to say nothing and let the other referees decide. Alternatively, you can say:

> The English seems fine to me (but I am not a native speaker).

11.17   Be careful of your own level of English and spelling

If, as a reviewer, you make a comment about the author's English, then you need to be careful about your own too, as it might undermine your credibility. It is generally a good idea to use where possible only standard phrases. A sentence such as *The English must profoundly to be enhanced* may indicate to the authors that your level of English is actually even worse than theirs. Also be careful of misspellings and inappropriate language:

> Figure 4 sounds wired to me—why is the resolution worst when does the flow rate increase?

The sentence above contains several mistakes: *sounds* should be *looks* (a figure is something you look at not listen to); *wired* should be *weird* (i.e., strange, but *weird* itself is a very colloquial word); and *worst* (superlative) should be *worse*; the last part of the sentence should read *when the flow rate increases* (*why* is the question word not *when*).

Also be very careful when making comments about the English that you don't make mistakes yourself as this will undermine your credibility both for the editor and the authors. Here are some examples with the mistakes highlighted in italics.

> *English need* to be corrected by an *en*glish speaker

> The *orgnization* and writing of the paper *need to improve*. There are some grammar errors *need to correct.*

> I would *suggest the authors to* have some *native English speaking* to go through it

> If the paper is accepted, I strongly recommend *an* English *prof*-reading.

Rev 1: The paper is generally well written (the English is good)

Rev 2: *A proof reading by a mother tongue* would improve readability.

Note: The above were taken from http://shitmyreviewerssay.tumblr.com/

11.18   My plea to referees with regard to author's level of English

I would like to make my own plea to referees, particularly to non-native referees. I have seen many many papers that were initially rejected due to "poor English." These comments were made by referees <u>after</u> I and other colleagues had corrected the English of the paper in question. Clearly, there may have been a few errors that myself and my proofreaders missed or that were introduced by the authors as they made their final modifications. But the errors were rarely enough to justify rejection. Since I am an English teacher I have no difficulty in spotting whether the comments come from referees who are native or non-native speakers. Virtually all come from non-native referees.

If you are convinced that the errors are in sufficient quantity and sufficiently serious to impede an understanding of the paper, then of course it is legitimate to draw the editor's and the authors' attention to this fact.

However, please bear in mind the following:

- Having a paper proofread costs a lot of money. Funds for research are getting increasingly lower, and in some parts of the world are virtually non-existent. If you unnecessarily ask for a revision of the English, you are costing researchers time and money that would probably be better spent on research.

- If you find two or three banal errors such as *in literature* rather than *in the literature*, or *it was founded that* rather than *it was found that*, do not conclude that the rest of the paper contains many more examples of this type (it may do, and if so you should tell the authors; but it may not—so check).

- Spelling mistakes are also made by native speakers, for example: *catagory* (instead of the correct spelling: category), *definately* (definitely), *equiptment* (equipment), *foriegn* (foreign), *fullfill* (fulfill), *goverment* (government), *maintainence* (maintenance), *neccessary* (necessary), *relevent* (relevant), and *transfered* (transferred). Native speakers also frequently confuse *they're*, *there*, and *their*; *its* and *it's*. So if, as I suspect, native speakers are rarely, if ever, criticized for there (sorry their) English, think twice before criticizing a non-native.

If you are a native speaker it may be tempting to criticize another researcher's English, but remember that unlike you they will have spent years learning English. In Italy, where I live and work, I have calculated that many academics spend around €10,000 to learn English, and an average of €150 per paper to have it corrected. These are costs that native speakers do not have to sustain and should not unnecessarily impose on their non-native colleagues.

Having said all this, if you think sloppy English and sloppy spelling may be indicative of a sloppy methodology and thus of sloppy data, then of course you should mention this in your report.

Chapter 12

Writing a Reply to the Reviewers' Reports

What the experts say

If the report is not what you were hoping for and seems needlessly critical, it is best to delay sending an email expressing your reaction. Instead, wait a few days, and then go back to it. Firstly, this allows your initial anger and demoralization to subside, and secondly when you re-read the report you may actually find something useful in it. Clearly, if you ask someone to do an informal review for you, it is not wise to then be critical of what they say. Thus your strategy is similar to the one you would adopt when you receive a referee's report from a journal: the referee is merely an obstacle to getting your paper accepted, so learn from him / her, and do whatever you can to say something positive about their suggestions, and then implement them into your manuscript. A few months' later you will not even be able to remember what changes you made and why you had to make them— all you will remember is the satisfaction of seeing your manuscript published.

Brian Martin, Professor of Social Sciences at the University of Wollongong, Australia, author of Surviving Referees' Reports

I have trained hundreds of graduate students, and see a consistent pattern in the things they find difficult. Most notably, graduate students have usually been trained and selected for their technical skills, not their emotional intelligence, and often have to develop communication skills on their own. This means that when faced with sharp, anonymous feedback of the sort that can appear in referee comments, they're often at a loss as to how to respond. Developing the ability to maintain a self-aware, positive approach under these circumstances is at least as important for academic careers as it is in business.

Alex Lamb, Alex Lamb Training, trainer in empowerment for those in the worlds of academia and business

In my work as an editor of scientific articles, I have read dozens of replies to referees reports. Clearly, as an author you should not simply accept everything the referees say. But when you give your reasons for such non acceptance it always pays to do so in a constructive way, without attempting to call into question the reputation, expertise or knowledge of the referee. My advice would be to wait at least 24 hours before hitting the "send" button—this enables you to vent your anger on one day, and then go back to remove all signs of that anger the next day.

Anna Southern, editor, English for Academics

© Springer International Publishing Switzerland 2016
A. Wallwork, *English for Academic Correspondence*,
English for Academic Research, DOI 10.1007/978-3-319-26435-6_12

12.1　What's the buzz?

Your paper is likely to be reviewed by two or three experts (known as reviewers or referees - see Chapter 11). Your reply to the editor of the journal regarding the reviewers' comments is also known as a 'rebuttal'.

Look at the beginning of two letters to the editor below. In both cases the manuscript in question was reviewed by three experts.

- How do you think the editor reacted?

- In what ways could you improve what the authors wrote?

LETTER A: Let us first thank the reviewers #2 and #3 for their contribution. Their suggestions were very useful during the revision process and have been incorporated into the revised manuscript. They helped us to understand the weak points of the paper and, as a result, we believe the quality of the revised paper has been significantly improved.

LETTER B: We are highly disappointed by reviewer 3's comments which appear to us biased and unfair. He / She has the right to disapprove of a paper but, in our opinion, most of the comments do not match the content of the paper or are false. The positive and constructive comments from the other reviewers are the best answer to him / her.

****

I have read hundreds of replies to referees reports and in my experience the approach in the letters above is very dangerous. Your objective is ONLY to have your paper published. You should not irritate or insult the referee in any way.

- start with something that you agree with about what the reviewer has said (this makes the reviewer and editor feel happy and will make them more likely to accept what you say afterwards)

- say what you want to say in a less critical manner which gives the reviewer some benefit of the doubt, but which still enables you to justify yourself

Brian Martin, Professor of Social Sciences at the University of Wollongong, Australia, writes:

It's helpful to treat referees' comments as part of an obstacle course. Your goal is to publish your work and communicate it to readers. Getting past the referees is something you need to do to get to the goal, and, as a bonus, you might improve your work along the way. So, rather than dwelling on the criticisms, it's more productive to proceed systematically in making revisions.

I suspect, though I have no hard data to support this suspicion, that revised papers that might have been accepted for publication are sometimes rejected because of the negative and antagonistic stance taken by the authors when addressing the reviewers' comments. This chapter describes how to respond to the criticisms and opinions of the reviewers without either being rude or obsequious. The result will be to increase the chances of your manuscript being published.

In this chapter you will learn that:

* your prime aim should be to have your paper published rather than to protect your pride
* the tone of your reply may have a big impact on whether your paper is accepted
* it generally makes sense to do what the reviewers suggest

12.2 Remember that yours is not the first paper to have been rejected

Research by Juan Miguel Campanario and presented in his paper *Have referees rejected some of the most-cited articles of all times?* shows that authors of some key papers encountered 'difficulty or resistance in doing or publishing' their research.

As authors we often associate the rejection of our paper with some kind of personal rejection. In reality it is perfectly normal and right for papers to be rejected (subject to changes). This is how science works. You get judged by our peers, and in the process receive a lot of useful advice. The secret is to separate your anger from your sense of objectivity.

12.3 Structure your reply to the referees in a way that will keep referees and editors happy

If you want to increase the chances of having your paper accepted for publication, then you might like to try the following four-stage strategy.

First, try to find something about what the referee has said that you can agree with

> The referee is certainly right when he / she says that …

> I thank the referee for pointing out that …

> I agree with the referee's comments about …

> We have implemented the referee's useful observations about …

Such phrases do not undermine the referee's credibility or their feeling of importance. They will feel that their expertise has been taken into account.

Second, tell the referee that you have amended something that they mentioned.

> Referee 1 suggested providing more complete results. This was a very useful suggestion, so we have now applied the proposed method to a typical industrial application (see the new Section 5).

Third, now that the referee is happy, you can tell him / her why you didn't amend something else.

> Given that the paper is intended for a broad audience, we decided not to cut the first two paragraphs of the Introduction.

Fourth, if possible, finish with something else positive about the referee's comments.

> We would like to thank the referee once more for sparing the time to write so many detailed and useful comments.

12.4 Present your answers to the reviewers using the clearest possible layout

I have seen many different ways to structure the reply to the reviewers. The best ones are those that help both the referees and the editors to understand what changes have been made and where.

Deal with each referee's report individually. If the referee has numbered his / her comments and queries, then the simplest solution is to paste in your responses under each comment. For example:

REFEREE 1

page 4, line 2: there is no clear connection between the two sentences.

The sentences have been clarified as follows: …

page 5, paragraph 3: this paragraph adds no value, I think it could be deleted

Done.

page 7, last line: What does "intervenes in the process" mean in this context?

We have replaced "intervene in" with "affects the process." NB this line now appears at the top of page 8.

Note how the author has put all the referees' comments in italics, and his own replies in normal script. This avoids rather ugly and redundant solutions such as:

Referee: 1) page 4, line 2: there is no clear connection between the two sentences.

Author: The sentences have been clarified as follows: ...

Or even worse:

Answer to referee's comment No. 3) page 7, last line: What does "intervenes in the process" mean in this context?

WE HAVE REPLACED "INTERVENE IN" WITH "AFFECTS THE PROCESS."

The use of capital letters is particularly unattractive and is also more difficult to read than lower case script.

Sometimes referees do not indicate line or page numbers but simply write unreferenced comments in one long paragraph or in a series of paragraphs. If there is just one long paragraph, the best solution is to divide up the paragraph into paragraphs of three to four lines, and then paste your comments directly below each of the resulting sub-paragraphs.

The example below shows the referee's comment, again changed to italics by the author. This is followed by the author's response (in normal script), with pages and line references indicated where appropriate.

The experimental procedure is not sufficiently informative to allow replication. How was the overall procedure carried out? The author should explain the procedure in detail or cite a reference. Was this procedure applied to the whole sample or just to a part of it? In addition, the instruments for determining X and Y should be reported.

We agree with the referee's comment regarding replication. On page 6 we have inserted a reference to one of our previous papers that contains a detailed description of the total digestion procedure. We have specified that it is applied just to the elutriate. Regarding the two instruments, in the original manuscript we had in fact stated what they were, but in a different section. So we have now moved these statements to a more logical position in the Materials section (page 5, second paragraph).

A possible structure in both cases—with or without page and line numbering—is thus:

1. Optional: General comments on all the referees' reports but without comments on specific reports.

2. Comments on Referee 1, then comments on Referee 2, then comments on Referee 3. Where necessary, include old and new line and page numbering to help the referees and editors see where you have made the changes.

3. Final overall comments.

12.5   Be brief

Try not to write unnecessarily long explanations for things that you could say very quickly. For example, the following sentence:

> I greatly appreciate the fact that the referee highlighted the English mistakes. I really need this because I am not a native English speaker. In the new version of the paper I have fixed all the mistakes that the referee reported.

Could be rewritten more succinctly as:

> The English has been revised [by a professional mother tongue speaker].

12.6   Call yourselves *we* not *the authors*

Referring to yourselves as "the authors" is not only artificial but creates strange sentences such as:

> *The authors* were pleased that the paper was appreciated. With regard to the referees' concerns about the procedure, *they* have tried to explain it in more detail …

If you call yourselves "the authors" then you are forced to use "they" as a personal pronoun to refer to yourselves. In addition to this sounding very strange (it sounds like you are writing the response to the referees on behalf of some other authors), it can also be ambiguous—who does *they* refer to in the extract above—the authors or the referees? A much easier, logical, and less artificial solution is to use *we*:

> *We* were pleased that the paper was appreciated. With regard to the referees' concerns about the procedure, *we* have tried to explain *our* procedure in more detail …

12.7 Don't be embarrassed to say you don't understand the referee's comments

Sometimes the referee may make some comments that appear to make no sense. In such cases, you can write:

Unfortunately, we were not able to understand this comment.

We are not sure what the referee means here.

It is not clear, in our opinion, what the referee is referring to.

12.8 Use the present and present perfect to outline the changes you have made

When you tell the editor what changes you have made to your manuscript, you will mainly use three tenses. Use the

- present perfect to describe the changes

  We have reduced the Abstract to 200 words.

  We have given names to each section.

- present simple to talk about how the manuscript looks now

  The Abstract is now only 200 words long.

  Sections are now referred to by name.

- simple past to talk about decisions

  We decided to keep the tables because ...

When you talk about things that you didn't change, you can use either the present perfect or the simple past.

We have kept / kept Figure 1 because ...

The above are not rules but merely what I have observed from reading many replies to referees' reports.

12.9   Justify why and where you have not made changes

The editor will be interested just as much in the recommended changes that you did not make as much as those that you did make. If you decided not to make a change, then you need to justify your decision. Here are some examples—the referees' recommendations are in italics, and the authors' responses are in normal script.

> *Remove Table 1 it contains no new information.*

> We have kept Table 1 as we believe it does contain important information. In fact, in the second column we report the values of … In addition, the third column shows … We believe it is important for the reader to see these values in tabular form as they give a very clear visual comparison of the various approaches.

> *The appendix can be deleted; it serves no purpose other than unnecessarily extending the length of the paper.*

> Although we agree with the referee that the paper is rather long, we believe that the appendix is vital for those readers who …

> *The authors have failed to provide details of the procedure for x.*

> These details are in fact provided in Ref. 2 (see page 6, line 17); for the sake of space we did not reproduce them in the current manuscript.

12.10   If you disagree with the reviewers, always be diplomatic

I suggest avoiding the use of the verb *disagree* and, if possible, minimize the use of adverbs such as *but, although, moreover, despite this, nevertheless,* and *in fact* where such adverbs are used to contradict what the referee has said. This should help your cause and will not draw attention to the fact that you are not in agreement.

REFEREE'S COMMENT	UNDIPLOMATIC RESPONSE	DIPLOMATIC RESPONSE
There is a lack of any innovative contribution.	We do not agree at all. Moreover, we have not found any examples of a similar contribution in the literature.	Having read the comment about lack of an innovative contribution, we rechecked the literature and could find no examples of anyone having used this method before. We believe that our work really is innovative for the following reasons:
Some of the results are misleading.	If Ref 1 had taken the time to read the whole paper, he / she would have seen that in Sect 4 we argue that the results were unexpected.	The referee certainly has a point in terms of x and y (which we have now corrected). Also, see Section 4, where we argue that the results were unexpected.
The results are incomplete.	Incomplete in what sense?	We understand what the referee is saying. We thought that we had covered all aspects, but on the basis of the referee's comment we have added a short case study to indicate the completeness of our results.
Cut Table 1—it repeats much of what is already in the text.	Although there is some repetition we disagree with the referee; in fact we think it is essential for reader comprehension.	We appreciate that Table 1 repeats some of what is already in the text, but in our experience this kind of table significantly helps readers to understand the concepts better.
The Conclusions are almost the same as the Abstract.	The referee may have a point; however, we have read many other papers published in the Journal, even by native speakers of English, which adopt exactly the same technique.	The referee is right and we have made several changes to ensure that the Conclusions are different from the Abstract, by · talking about possible applications · mentioning future work

I am not advocating simply accepting all the referee's comments, especially if they are clearly misguided. All I am saying is to do what you think is best, but to describe what you have done in the most diplomatic way possible so that the editor will be more inclined to accept what you have done.

The last example highlights the fact that if you have made a mistake you should admit it—don't try to justify the unjustifiable!

12.11 If a reviewer finds a limitation in your work, deal with the criticism constructively

One of the main tasks of a reviewer / referee of papers is to find any limitations (from a scientific point of view) in your work. In doing so, the reviewers are not trying to destroy your work but rather they are inviting you to rethink your work and make improvements.

Sometimes you will agree with their comments but you feel there is nothing you can do to make amends for your limitation. In these cases you will have to offer a counter-argument or justification, which is sometimes referred to as a 'rebuttal'.

For example, a reviewer might write "The authors should consider investigating data on X".

In your reply to the editor you could write one or more of the following:

> We were unable to access the data on X because such data are not available in the public domain.

> Other studies found the same problem (e.g. Lu 2015, King 2017) and such authors thus decided to focus only on Y and Z.

> We are currently in the process of collecting data on X, and this will be the subject of a future paper.

However, you also need to adjust the text in your paper to take account of the reviewer's comment - if a reviewer wonders why you did not investigate X, then your readers might also wonder.

For instances, you could insert the third sentence above into your conclusions. By doing so you:

- admit that you have a limitation (no data on X)

- justify it by saying you are aware of the problem and actively engaging in resolving it

12.12 Don't find things to criticize in the referee's work or in the workings of the journal

When someone has spent several pages criticizing your work, it is often a natural reaction to find something to criticize in their work too. Below are three examples of how <u>not</u> to refer to the reviewers:

> EXAMPLE 1 I would also like to mention that Reviewer 3 seems rather superficial in his report, at least in the second part where he suggests that I should consider "other..... books…, e.g. by Wilkins or Guyot," without any other reference data—I find such remarks extremely unhelpful.

> EXAMPLE 2 Reviewer 2 seems to be questioning my background and my level of expertise in the research area. I demand to know who has dared to assume the responsibility of making derogatory comments violating the integrity of a fellow academic. I pity your journal—why do you select people like this to humiliate other professionals? I will not hesitate to inform the community of your journal's practice.

One of the messages that I hope to get across in this book is that you should never forget what your main aim is. Your main aim in this case is to get your paper published.

In the second example, singling out Reviewer 2 for condemnation is not a good approach and will not improve your chances of publication. It is highly likely that after reading the above response, Reviewer 2 will NOT change his (or her) position—in fact the laws of human nature dictate that he is likely to be more convinced than ever of his original position. In addition, you cannot be sure that Reviewer 2 is not a personal friend of the editor.

> EXAMPLE 3 We are highly disappointed by the reviewer's comments that appear to us biased and unfair. He is legitimate to disapprove a paper but, in our opinion, most of the comments do not match the content of the paper or are false (e.g. the paper contains only 8% devoted to actual work description, whereas it results over 70% from our calculation). The positive and constructive comments from the other reviewers are the best answer to him. Nevertheless, we acknowledge that the English and the reference section could be improved so we have worked on that and the paper has undergone a thorough revision by a mother tongue professional, as recommended by the reviewer.

It is part of human nature for authors to get annoyed by reviewers. Most authors would be annoyed by Reviewer 2's calculation of 7% (not 10% or an expression such as "most"), but there is nothing to be gained by imitating his / her style.

The problems with the above version are:

- immediate expression of the authors' emotions (*highly disappointed*) - this is of no value to the editor

- totally subjective opinion of the reviewer (*biased and unfair*) - given that the editor will have spent time choosing the reviewer, this opinion is also an indirect insult to the editor by calling into question his choice of reviewer

- use of the male pronoun *(he)* - reviewers are generally anonymous, so the authors cannot know if the reviewer was male or female. In the Anglo-Saxon world the use of he as a generic pronoun is considered wrong and by some also offensive

- use of the word *false* - this is very very strong

- use of sarcasm *(The positive and constructive comments from the other reviewers are the best answer to him)*

Below are two different ways of rewriting the third example in order to avoid compromising the chances of your paper being published.

REVISED VERSION 1 (RV1)	REVISED VERSION 2 (RV2)
First of all, we acknowledge, as the second reviewer correctly noted, that the English and the reference section needed improvement. We have now fixed the references and the paper has undergone a thorough revision by a mother tongue professional. However, we are a little perplexed by the reviewer's comments on the amount of the paper devoted to actual work descriptions. We have thought of ways of addressing this problem, but in any case we believe that in reality about 70% of the paper is dedicated to work descriptions—and this would seem to be confirmed by the positive and constructive comments from the other two reviewers.	We would firstly like to thank all the reviewers for their contribution. With regard to Reviewer 2's comment about the amount of space we have dedicated to the main topic, where possible we have tried to focus more on the topic. As also recommended by Reviewer 2, we have had the English reviewed by a mother tongue professional.

The strategy of RV1 is to

- start with something that you agree with about what the reviewer has said (this makes the reviewer and editor feel happy and makes them feel more positive about what you say afterwards)

- say what you want to say in a less critical manner which gives the reviewer some benefit of the doubt, but which still enables you to justify yourself

- modify any statements that you make that may be open to interpretation by saying *we believe / we hope / we think / in our opinion* or using conditionals (e.g., *would seem*)

The difference between RV1 and RV2 is that RV1 still risks irritating Reviewer 2 as it uses the word *perplexed* and then uses the support of Reviewers 1 and 3 to call into question what Reviewer 2 has said. This is also not helped by the reference to 70%.

In my opinion RV2 solves the problem by saying *where possible we have tried to focus more on the topic*. This is the perfect solution because it makes Reviewer 2 think that there was some truth in what he was saying (even if in reality there was no truth). At the same time it says that the authors have in some way implemented what Reviewer 2 suggested, though cleverly they don't mention how or where. This means that all parties are now happy. RV2 also has the advantage of being shorter.

The secret is not to call into question the reputation, professionalism, and expertise of any of the reviewers. Insulting the referee almost invariably leads to your paper being rejected.

If your reaction is to react heatedly or violently to the referee's reports, then it is best to write your response but then leave it for a few days. During those few days you will probably find that there is some truth in what the referee says, and that you may have overreacted because you were hoping to have your paper published straight away without any delays for revisions.

I strongly suggest that when you have written your reply, go through it very carefully and delete any sentences that might offend, even minimally, the referee. Such sentences add nothing to your quest of getting your paper published. All they do is to irritate the referee in question, and shed doubt on the editor's ability to choose a competent referee. They also preclude your chances of ever publishing in that journal again.

12.13   Be aware of what might happen if you ignore the referee's advice

Researchers are rarely satisfied with the reviews they receive. It can be a very disappointing (and unfortunately sometimes humiliating) experience to read a review that either rejects your manuscript completely or apparently requires too many changes for you to realistically make.

The secret is to try not to take the reviewer's comments personally, but to see them as sincere advice on how to improve your manuscript. Clearly, on some occasions referees totally misunderstand your paper. But often their misunderstanding is due to the fact that you have not expressed yourself clearly or because you have not really highlighted your results and their importance.

If you choose to ignore the referee's advice, particularly when it has been given to you in a constructive manner, then you risk receiving a second report from the referee, such as the following one:

> I very much appreciate the authors' efforts to meet the referees' requirements. However, I have re-read their new version several times to convince myself that may be I had reached the wrong conclusions in my previous assessment. Despite this I am now more convinced than ever that the paper cannot be accepted. The manuscript is still confusing for the reader. The complexity of the topic does not justify the excessive length of the manuscript nor the excessive number of tables and figures.
>
> In my previous report I suggested the authors should (i) try to be clear and concise in describing their aims and methods, (ii) present their most important relevant findings through an appropriate selection of significant data, and (iii) ensure that their Discussion and Conclusions reflected the data.
>
> Unfortunately, the authors chose to ignore my suggestions, and consequently their manuscript is not substantially different now from its original version.
>
> Consequently, I regret having to recommend that this manuscript should not be accepted for publication. This is a real shame as it contains much data of interest to the community, and also adopts a novel approach.

The above report indicates that the reviewer had no problem with the scientific content itself, but just in the way that the data were presented. He was concerned with a basic lack of readability and for that reason rejected the paper. It would not have been so difficult for the authors to have appeased the referee's concerns by making their paper easier to read.

Chapter 13

Communicating with the Editor

What the experts say

I have been editor and guest editor of many scientific journals. As an editor I always try to establish a good relation with all the researchers / authors who wish to publish their work. It very much eases the publishing process if the authors adopt a constructive approach, both in their responses to reviewers and in the cover letter to the editor. Clearly, the most important thing for an editor to do is to judge the scientific merit of a paper. However, editors are human, and as such they are affected, consciously or subconsciously, by any negative or aggressive stance taken by the author.

Luciano Lenzini, Professor, Department of Information Engineering,
University of Pisa, Italy

The cover letter is the first step to getting your article published. A poorly written letter containing grammatical and / or spelling mistakes will not make a good first impression and may affect how the editor subsequently reads your paper. Also, remember that you are not necessarily doing the journal a favor by sending them your manuscript. You need to convince the editor of the importance of your work. Use as few a words as possible: editors receive maybe a hundred emails a day and don't normally appreciate lengthy explanations. If you always try to see things from the editor's point of view and make life simple for them, then that will certainly help your chances.

Mark Worden, editor, Speak Up

Over my long career as an author a lesson that I have learned, which I would like to pass on to first time authors, is always to be diplomatic with your editor. Editors have a tough job, and it pays to be appreciative of what they do. Essentially, your main aim is to get your work published as quickly as possible. Anything you can do to smooth this process will help you in this objective. Be diplomatic at all times, even if you are in strong disagreement. Always do everything you can to appreciate, and if possible accommodate, their point of view.

Keith Harding, ELT author and trainer

© Springer International Publishing Switzerland 2016
A. Wallwork, *English for Academic Correspondence*,
English for Academic Research, DOI 10.1007/978-3-319-26435-6_13

13.1   What's the buzz?

1) Imagine that you submitted your paper for publication in a journal several months ago. The editor has never replied even though you have written him / her two emails.

Write an email following the three instructions below:

1. Think of a subject line.
2. Explain the situation and ask whether your paper has been accepted or not.
3. Use appropriate salutations at the beginning and end.

2) Now look at the email below. Apart from the various mistakes in the English, what other problems can you see

Subject line: Paper submission

Dear Sir

My name is Pinco Pallino and I submitted my paper to you several months ago and I am still waiting for your judge.

This is the third email I write to know if my paper was admitted or not. Please answer me in any case.

Best regards

****

As you will have seen from what the experts say (see previous page), it is vital not to underestimate the importance of establishing and maintaining a positive relationship with your editor. This chapter shows you how to do that and thus improve your chances of having your research published. The chapter highlights the importance of

- the cover letter in affecting the outcome of your paper

- not saying anything negative about the editor and the journal

13.2 Focus only on what you need to achieve

The problem with the Pinco Pallino's email (see 13.1) is that instead of increasing your chances of having your paper published you have decreased them. This is because you have

- used a completely generic subject line—an editor's primary work is dealing with paper submissions, so this kind of subject line is very unhelpful

- not taken the trouble to find out the name of the editor

- criticized (explicitly and implicitly) the editor—what kind of person doesn't answer three emails?

- showed the editor that your English is poor; therefore he / she might conclude that if the English in your email is poor, then there is a good chance that it will be poor in the paper too

A much better version would be

Subject line: Paper submission Manuscript 1453

Dear Helena Smith

I was wondering if you had received my email sent 14 September (see below) regarding the submission of my manuscript (1453).

Please find attached a copy of the paper for your convenience.

Best regards

The above is much better because it thinks about the editor's point of view. You provide

- a meaningful subject line

- the name of the editor

- all the info the editor needs + you save him / her time by attaching another copy of the paper and by incorporating your original email at the end of the current one

In addition, there is absolutely no sense of criticism. You are aware that the editor may have had more important things to do than reply to your email. After all, he / she is doing you a favor if he / she publishes your paper. You are not doing him / her a favor by sending your paper (unless you are already a Nobel prize winner!).

13.3 Ensure your cover email / letter is clear and accurate

Writing a good cover email / letter is crucial in increasing the chances of your paper being published. It will be the first example of your writing skills that the Editor sees. If it is clear and accurate, then the Editor may also make the assumption that your manuscript is equally clear and that your data are accurate. If however it is poorly structured and contains mistakes in the English, this might condition the Editor's expectations with regard to your manuscript. Below is an example of a good cover letter.

Dear Professor Seinfeld

I would like to submit for publication in the *Journal of Future Education* the attached paper entitled *A Proposal for Radical Educational Reform* by Adrian Wallwork and Anna Southern.

Our aim was to test the efficiency of short vs long degree courses. Our study of 15,000 male and female graduates aged between 35 and 55 found that they would have performed far better in their careers from a financial point of view if they had undertaken a one-year course at university rather than the traditional three- to four-year course.

Our key finding is that people on shorter courses will earn up to 15% more during their lifetime. The implications of this are not only for the graduates themselves but also for governments as i) governments could save considerable amounts of money and ii) universities would be free to accept more students.

We believe that our findings will be of great interest to readers of your journal, particularly due to their counterintuitive nature and the fact they go against the general trend that claims that university courses should be increased in length.

This research has not been published before and is not being considered for publication elsewhere.

I look forward to hearing from you.

The structure and content of the above letter and many of the recommendations below are based on advice given on the *British Medical Journal's* website (http://resources.bmj.com/bmj/pdfs/wager.pdf):

- Find out the name of the current editor, rather than simply writing *Dear Sir / Madam*. This shows that you have made an effort, which reflects the fact that you are serious about getting your paper published in their journal

- Ensure that the editor's name is spelt correctly (e.g., *Seinfeld* rather than *Sienfled*). No one likes to see their name misspelled

- Ensure that the journal's name is spelt correctly and is the correct one (be careful of using old cover letters, you may forget to delete old information)

- Provide a brief summary of the aim and outcome of the research (paragraph 2 in the above example)

- Outline the key findings and the implications (paragraph 3)

- State why readers of the journal will be interested in your findings and how it fits in with recent articles in the journal (paragraph 4).

- Reassure the editor that his / her journal has an exclusive on your manuscript (paragraph 5)

If you have had your paper revised by a professional proofreader, send him / her your cover letter to check as well

If you are writing to a non-specialized journal such as *Nature* or *Scientific American*, then you need to convince the editor that your paper is topical, that it will interest a non-scientific audience, and that an interdisciplinary journal is a more suitable form of publication for your research than a single-discipline or archival journal.

In both cases—specialized and non-specialized—make sure you read the instructions for the author on their websites, which often give instructions not only regarding the manuscript but also about the cover letter.

13.4   If you've only made a few changes, describe them in the letter to the editor

If the reviewer has only asked for minor changes, and if you can describe these changes in around 20 lines or less, then you can incorporate these changes directly into the letter to the editor.

> Dear Professor Seinfeld
>
> Please find attached the revised manuscript (No. FE 245.998 Ver 2) by *names of authors*. Following the reviewers' comments, we have made the following changes: …
>
> There was only one change (suggested by Ref. 2) that was not made, which was to delete Figure 2. We decided to retain Figure 2 for the following two reasons: …
>
> I hope you will find the revised manuscript suitable for publication in *name of journal*.
>
> Best regards

If your replies to the reviewers take up more than one page, then they should be written in a separate document. In this case you can write:

> Please find attached the revised manuscript (No. FE 245.998 Ver 2) by *names of authors*. Also attached are our responses to the reviewers, including all the changes that have been made.

13.5 Mention whether the manuscript has already been revised by a native speaker

Unfortunately some papers get 'rejected subject to review' due to poor English, when in fact the English is absolutely fine (see 11.16 and 11.18). This is because some non-native reviewers seem to feel obliged to protect themselves by saying the English needs revising because they themselves are unable to judge the level of English, or perhaps because they spotted a mistake in the Abstract and assumed that if there was a mistake in the Abstract then there would likely be mistakes in the rest of the manuscript too.

To avoid such comments by referees you can write one of the following:

> The paper has been edited and proofread by Rupert Burgess, one of the co-authors of the paper who is a native English speaker.

> The paper has been edited and proofread by a professional native English speaking editing service.

If you have used an editing service, get them to send you a certificate that they have edited your paper. You can then forward this certificate to the editor.

Adopting these solutions should speed up the process of getting your paper published.

Alexander (Sandy) Lang, founder / director of Rescript, a professional editing service, says:

> Having your manuscript revised by a professional editing service prior to journal submission will greatly improve the quality of its English – both the grammar and also the readability. Additionally, if the editor has experience as a researcher and is familiar with your discipline, then minor technical errors can also be corrected at this stage. Overall, your work will then create a much better impression with the journal referees, thus reducing the number of their criticisms and misunderstandings, and increasing the chances of its acceptance for publication.

13.6 Be diplomatic in any emails to check the progress of your manuscript

Your manuscript is very important to you and you will obviously want it to be published as soon as possible with the minimal amount of trouble.

However, your manuscript is far more important to you than it is to an editor who may be handling 50 or 60 manuscripts at a time.

If you have submitted a manuscript and you have not heard from the editor for three months, then it is certainly a good idea to check what is happening. The email below shows how <u>not</u> to do this.

> Dear Professor Carling,
>
> On January 14 of this year I submitted a manuscript (ID 09-00236) entitled *name of paper* for possible publication in *name of journal*. On March 14 I was informed that the paper had been accepted with MINOR REVISIONS. On April 3, I resubmitted my manuscript (ID 09-00236.R1), revised according to the Editor's and Referees' comments.
>
> So far, more than THREE months after submitting the revised manuscript, I haven't received any news about the final decision.
>
> Given that:
>
> - nowadays most journals have reduced their publication times
>
> - the paper was accepted on the basis of only minor revisions
>
> - I submitted the revised manuscript strictly following the suggestions of the Referees
>
> it seems reasonable to wonder what the reasons are for this unexpected and unusual delay.
>
> I look forward to hearing from you.

Basically, the email above (which is absolutely genuine apart from the names and ID numbers) could have been rewritten as *Dear Editor, You are an incompetent imbecile. You have had my paper for more than three months—do you want to publish it or not?*

You have absolutely no idea for the reasons in the delay in the final decision regarding your manuscript. Perhaps the editor has

- been replaced with a new editor

- had serious family problems

- had problems with his PC and has lost your email and / or manuscript

- still not received a reply from one of the reviewers despite chasing this reviewer three times

The email above would be particularly irritating for the editor because

- it does not attempt to see things at all from her point of view

- the use of capitals is extremely impolite

- the use of the numbered bullets and the content of these bullets is completely unnecessary

- it contains many unnecessary details (e.g., the chronology of events)

- it has an aggressive and sarcastic tone

Your aim should simply be to get your paper published not to express negative comments on the way the journal carries out its activities.

Also, remember that writing in another language often acts as a filter and you may not be able to judge either the level of aggression in what you have written or the kind of reaction you might receive. A much better approach, which does not compromise the establishment of good relationships, is the following:

> I wonder if you could help me with a problem.
>
> On April 3 of this year, I resubmitted my manuscript (ID 09-00236.R1), revised according to the Editor's and Referees' comments.
>
> I am just writing to check whether there is any news about the final decision. As you can see from the attached emails below, I have in fact raised this problem twice before.
>
> Anything you could do to speed the process up would be very much appreciated.
>
> Thank you very much in advance.

The revised email above contains the same information as the original "aggressive" email, but presents this information in a friendly, professional, and non-aggressive way that will not make the editor feel either angry or guilty. Attaching the previous correspondence (*as you can see from the attached emails below*) enables you to give the editor clear evidence of what you are saying yet at the same time do so in a totally neutral way.

Another case is when your paper has already been accepted for publication, but since then you have had no news. The email below is successful in making this point because it reveals that the authors urgently need to see their paper published. It is also written in a clear and polite way. It makes reference to previous email communication between the editor and the authors by simply saying *see your email below* rather than insulting the editor for his/her incompetence.

Subject: Manuscript - #WTF-277

Dear Editor,

Our paper "Is the fact that the English language only has one form of the second person pronoun *you* indicative of more democratic society in Anglo countries?" written by Modou Diop and Haana Diagne, manuscript number WTF-277, was accepted for publication last April 04 (see your email below). However since then we have not received any further information about it.

As you will appreciate, we are concerned that there may be some problems in the publication process. The situation is rather urgent for us as we need the volume and page numbers of our paper in order to fill in official budget requests for our institutes.

We look forward to hearing from you.

Chapter 14

Useful Phrases

14.1 What's the buzz?

It is a good idea to keep a glossary where you can note down useful generic phrases that you receive in the emails sent to you by native English speakers. You can then 'paste' these into your own emails.

This chapter presents lists of frequently used phrases that have a general acceptance in all types of emails, not just in academia. This means that they are phrases that your recipients will frequently encounter.

The lists are not comprehensive and you should try to add other useful phrases that frequently occur in your field.

Phrases that are very formal are followed by an asterisk (*).

In this section, *you* and *your* refer to the person who wrote the original email, and *recipient* refers to the person who received the writer's email.

The phrases are punctuated as follows:

Where there is no punctuation at the end of the phrase, this means that typically native speakers use no punctuation. This is often the case with the initial and the

© Springer International Publishing Switzerland 2016   181
A. Wallwork, *English for Academic Correspondence*,
English for Academic Research, DOI 10.1007/978-3-319-26435-6_14

final salutation. However, in these cases, it would also be possible to use a comma. So it would be possible to write both of the following:

Dear Adrian

Dear Adrian,

Some writers also use a colon after the initial salutation. Example:

Dear Adrian:

A period (.) at the end of the phrase indicates that the phrase ends at this point.

Three dots (…) this means that the phrase would continue.

A colon (:) indicates that a list and / or comments would follow.

An interrogative mark (?) indicates that this is a question. Note that often phrases that begin "Can you …" or "Could you …" are not considered questions when they are simply a polite way of giving someone instructions. Examples:

Could you send the file by the end of today. Thanks.

Can you let me know as soon as possible.

Examples of real questions are those where the writer is expecting a reply to his / her question:

Can you speak English?

14.2   Initial salutation

Standard

Dear Alfred
Dear Alfred Einstein
Dear Dr Einstein
Dear Professor Einstein

To group / team

Dear all
Hi all
Hi everybody
To all members of the xxx group

To someone you know well

Hi!
Hope you are keeping well.
Hope all is well.

To someone / some people whose names or job positions you don't know

Hi
Hello
Good morning
To whom it may concern * *but try to find the name of the correct person*
Dear Sir / Madam * *but try to find the name of the correct person*

14.3   Final salutation

Neutral

Best regards
Kind regards
Best wishes
Regards

Informal

All the best
Have a nice weekend and I'll write when we're back.
See you on Friday.
Hope to hear from you soon.
Speak to you soon.
Cheers

Formal

With kind regards
With best wishes
Yours sincerely
Yours faithfully

14.4   Phrase before final salutation

Very informal excuses for ending

Must go now because ...
I've got to go now.
That's all for now.

Sending regards to other people

Say hello to ...
Please send my regards to ...
Please convey my best wishes to ... *

Wishing people well

Best wishes for the holidays and the new year from all of us here at …
Have a great Thanksgiving!
Have a nice weekend.
Happy Easter to everyone.
May I wish you a … *
I would like to take this opportunity to wish you a peaceful and prosperous New Year. *

14.5   Giving main reason for message

To known person or group of known people

Just a quick update on …
Just to let you know that …
This is just a quick message to …
This email is to inform you that …
For your information here is …
This is to let you know that …
Just a quick message to ask you whether …
I was just wondering whether …

First contact to unknown person

I found your name in the references of X's paper on …
I am writing to you because …
Your address was given to me by …
Your name was given to me by …
Your address was given to me by …

Making reference to previous mail / phone call / conversation

In relation to / With reference to / Regarding …
Further to our conversation of yesterday, …
Further to our recent meeting, …
As requested I am sending you …

Making reference to previous meeting at conference

You may remember we met last year ...
You may recall that we met at the conference in Beijing ...

Following up telephone call

Thanks for ringing me yesterday.
It was good to speak to you this morning.
As I said / mentioned on the phone ...
I just wanted to check that I've got the details correctly.
With reference to our phone call of ... *formal* *
Re our phone call this morning ...
Further to our telephone conversation, here are the details of what we require.
Many thanks for your earlier call. As discussed, details as below:

14.6   Organizing content

Stressing main points and drawing attention to something

What I really want to stress here is ...
The important thing is ...
The key factor is ...
Can I draw your attention to ...
What I need to know is ...
It is crucial for me to ...
I cannot stress how important this is.

Indicating change in subject

One more thing ...
While I remember ...
Before I forget ...
By the way ...
Also ...

Summarizing and concluding

So, just to summarize ...
So basically I am asking you two things. First, ... And second ...
If you could answer all three of my questions I would be most grateful.

14.7   Asking favors / giving help

Asking

I found your email address on the web, and am writing to you in the hope that you may be able to help me.
Please could you …
I was wondering if by any chance you …
I wonder if you might be able to help me.
I would be extremely grateful if you could …
Would you have any suggestions on how to …
It would be very helpful for me if I could pick your brains on …
I would like to ask your advice about …

Showing awareness that you are taking up recipient's time

I realize you must be very busy at the moment but if you could spare a moment I would be most grateful.
If it wouldn't take up too much of your time then I would be very grateful if you could …
Clearly, I don't want to take up too much of your time but if you could …
Obviously, I don't expect you to …. but any help you could give me would be much appreciated.

Accepting

No problem. I'll get back to you as soon as …
I'd be happy to help out with …
I'd be happy to help.

Declining

I'm sorry but …
I'd like to help but …
Unfortunately …
At the moment I'm afraid it's just not possible.

14.8   Invitations

Inviting

In accordance with our previous conversations, I am very glad to invite you to … *
I sincerely hope that you will be able to accept this invitation, and look forward to hosting you in *name of town*. *
I was wondering whether you might be interested in joining the Scientific Advisory Board of … *
I am writing to you to find out whether you would be willing to …

Accepting

Thank you very much for your kind invitation to … *
I would be delighted to be a member of … *
It is very kind of you to invite me to …

Declining

Many thanks for your kind invitation, but unfortunately …
I am really sorry but I am going to have to turn down your invitation to …
Thank you very much for your kind invitation. However, I am afraid that …
Thanks very much for inviting me to … I am really sorry but I am afraid I cannot accept.
I regret that I cannot accept your invitation at the present time because … *
I'm sorry to inform you that I do not have sufficient expertise in *topic* to be able to review the paper. *
So it is with great regret that I am afraid that I will have to decline your invitation. *

Withdrawing acceptance

I am sorry to have to inform you that I am no longer able to …
Due to family problems I am sorry to have to inform you that …
I am sorry to give you such short notice and I sincerely hope that this won't cause you too much trouble.

14.9   Making inquiries

General inquiries

Hi, I have a couple of simple requests:
Could you please tell me …
I would like to know …
Could you possibly send me …
I have some questions about …

Asking to receive papers

I would like to receive a copy of your PhD Thesis "Metalanguage in Swahili."
Last week I attended the workshop on X. I was interested in your presentation on
"Y." Have you by any chance written a paper on that topic? If so, I would very much
appreciate it if you could email me a copy.
I am a PhD student currently doing a review on the link between right-wing politics
and the perception of social justice and I am interested in your article "Social
Justice: Are you kidding?" I would much appreciate it if you could send me the
article if possible.

Ordering products, materials, chemicals, etc.

What do I need to do to order a …?
I would like to know if I can order an xxx directly from you …
I am looking for an xx. Do you have one in stock?

Ending an inquiry

Any information you could give me would be greatly appreciated.
Thanks in advance.
I look forward to receiving …

Following up an inquiry

Thank you for …
Would it be possible for you to send me a bit more information on …
Could you please describe what is included in the …

14.10   Replying to inquiries

Thanking

Thank you for contacting me …
I am pleased to hear that you found my paper / presentation / report / seminar useful …

Making reference

Regarding your queries about …
In response to your questions:
Here is the information you requested:
As requested, I am sending you …
Below you will find the answers to your questions …
With reference to your request for …
Following our telephone conversation about …

Asking for details

Before I can answer your questions, I need further details re the following:
Before I can do anything, I need …
Could you tell me exactly why you need x.

Adding details

Please note that …
I would like to point out that …
As far as I know …
I'd also like to take this opportunity to bring to your attention …
May I take this opportunity to …

Telling recipients they can ask for further info

Please feel free to email, fax, or call if you have any questions.
Any questions, please ask.
Hope this is OK. Please contact Helen if you need any further details.
If you need any further details do not hesitate to contact me.
Should you have any questions please let us know.
Please do not hesitate to contact us should you need any further clarifications.

Ending

Please let me know if this helps.
I hope to be able to give you a definite answer soon.
Once again, thank you for contacting me.

14.11   Talking about the next step

Telling recipient how you want them to proceed

Could you please go through the manuscript and make any revisions you think necessary.
Please have a look at the enclosed report and let me know what you think.
If you could organize the meeting for next Tuesday, I'll send everyone the details.

Telling recipient how you will proceed

Thanks for your mail. It will take me a while to find all the answers you need but I should be able to get back to you early next week.
Re your request. I'll look into it and send you a reply by the end of the week.
I will contact you when I return.
Sorry, but I'm actually going on holiday tomorrow, so I'm afraid I won't be able to get back to you for a couple of weeks.

Asking recipient how they want you to proceed

Do you want me to …?
Would you like me to …?
Shall I ..?.
Do we need to …?
Let me know whether …

14.12   Giving and responding to deadlines

Telling recipient by when you want a reply

I look forward to hearing from you in the near future / soon / before the end of the week.
Please could you get back to me by the end of today / this morning / as soon as possible.
I hope you can reply this morning so I can then get things moving before leaving tonight.
We would appreciate an early reply.
Please let me have your feedback by Friday so I can send you a draft schedule next week.
I know it is a very sharp deadline. So if you don't have time to answer my question, please don't worry about it.
Looking forward to your reply.

When you will reply

I should be able to send you the document tomorrow / within the next two days / first thing Thursday morning.
I'll get back to you before the end of the day.
I'm sorry but I won't be able to give you any response until …

Saying what you will do

I will send you all the details re … in due course.
With regard to your email dated …, I will talk to my colleagues and get back to you ASAP.

Saying what you've done

Given the new data that we now have available, we have …
I have made the following changes: …

Asking for confirmation if what you have done is acceptable

I hope that is OK—if not please raise with Mike.
Is that OK?

Asking to be kept informed

Please keep me informed of any developments.
Please keep me up to date.
Please let us know the outcome.

14.13   Chasing

Chasing your previous mail

Did you get my last message sent on … ?
I was wondering whether you had received my email (see below).
May we remind you that we are still awaiting your reply to our message dated … *
We would be grateful if you could reply as soon as possible.
Sorry, but given that I have not heard from you I am worried that I did not explain the situation clearly.

Empathizing with recipient

Hope this doesn't cause you any problems / too much trouble.
Sorry if this adds to your workload.
I know you must be very busy but …

Saying when you will be able to fulfill the request

I am afraid I won't be able to start work on it until next week.
I honestly don't know when I'll be able to find the time to do it.

Excusing yourself for not having fulfilled the request yet

I am sorry, but as I am sure you are aware, I have been extremely busy doing X, so
I haven't had time to do Y.
I am really sorry but I have been extremely busy.
It's been a really hectic week.
I've been snowed under with work.

14.14 Making arrangements for meetings and teleconferences

Suggesting the time

Let's arrange a call so that we can discuss it further.
Can we arrange a conference call for 15.00 on Monday 21 October?
Would it be possible for us to meet next Tuesday morning?
How about Wednesday straight after lunch?
The best days for me would be sometime between October 1 and 10, with a slight
preference for early in the week of the 6th. Please let me know if that would be
possible.

Informing of unavailability at that time

Would love to meet—but not this week! I can manage Nov 16 or 17, if either of
those would suit you.
I am afraid I won't be available either today or tomorrow. Would Thursday 11
March suit you? Either the morning or the afternoon would be fine for me. I'd be
grateful if you could let me know as soon as possible so I can make the necessary
arrangements.

Sorry but I can't make it that day.
Sorry but I'll be on holiday then.
I'm afraid I have another engagement on 22 April.
Thank you for your invitation to attend your technical meeting. However, I am unlikely to be able to attend as I have a lot of engagements that day.

Declining

Unfortunately, due to limited resources I am unable to accept your invitation to come to the meeting.
I regret that I will not be able to attend the meeting.

Changing the time

Sorry, can't make the meeting at 13.00. Can we change it to 14.00? Let me know.
Re our meeting next week. I am afraid something has come up and I need to change the time. Would it be possible on Tuesday 13 at 15.00?
We were due to meet next Tuesday afternoon. Is there any chance I could move it until later in the week? Weds or Thurs perhaps?

Confirming the time

The meeting is confirmed for Friday at 10:30 am Pacific time, 12:30 pm Central time. Please send any items you want to discuss, and I will send an agenda earlier in the morning.

Responding to confirmation of the time

I look forward to seeing you on 30 November.
OK, Wednesday, March 10 at 11.00. I look forward to seeing you then.
OK, I will let the others know.

Cancelling

I am extremely sorry, but I am afraid I will not be able to participate in the teleconference that was arranged for next week.
I am sorry to leave this so late, but it looks like I won't be able to make the conference call tomorrow.
Due to family problems I will not be able to …

14.15   Sending documents for informal revision

Explaining background

I am currently working on a paper that I would like to submit to …
The paper is the extension of the work that I …
The draft is still at quite an early stage.

Explaining reason for sending document to this specific person

Given your expertise, it would be great if you could take a look at …
I would really appreciate your input on this because …
I know that you have done a lot of research on this …

Requesting help

When you have a moment do you think you could … ?
Could you possibly …
If you get a chance could you …
Do you think you might be able to help me with …?
I'd be grateful if you could help us with …
Could you please check these comments and let us know if you still have any issues with …
I hear you may be able to help out with writing the paper.
Please have a look at the enclosed report and let me know what you think.

Giving specific instructions

It would be great if you could read all of Sections 3 and 4. However, if you are short of time, please just read the last two subsections of Section 4.
Please let me know if you see any need for additions or deletions.
Don't worry about any typos at the moment or minor inconsistencies in the notation.
If you have any comments on x they would be gratefully received.
Just think about general aspects, such as whether I have missed anything vital out, or my reasoning doesn't seem to be very logical.
I'm attaching the draft in two versions: a pdf of the complete manuscript, including the graphs, and a Word file of just the text—this is so that you can write any comments directly on the file using Track Changes.

Giving deadlines

I know this is a lot to ask, but as I am already behind schedule do you think you could give me your feedback by the end of next week?
I know you must be very busy but …
Once you have reviewed the document, please forward it to …

Resending documents

Sorry, but I inadvertently sent you the wrong document.
I have made a few changes to the manuscript. If you haven't already started work on it, please could you use this version instead. If you have already started, then please ignore the new version.

14.16   Receiving and commenting on documents for informal revision

Accepting to do revision

I would be pleased to read / revise your document for you.
I am happy to give you my input on the first draft.
I'd be happy to help out with editing some sections of the paper.
Thank you for sending the manuscript. I just had a quick glance at it, and it looks very promising.

Declining request to do revision

I am sorry but I am extremely busy at the moment.
I am afraid I simply don't have the time to …

Declining a request for help after an initial acceptance

I am writing to tell you that unfortunately I no longer have the time to …
This is because …
Once again my sincere apologies for this.
I am extremely sorry about this and I do hope it does not put you in any difficulty.

Saying when you could begin / complete the work

In the next couple of days I will go through it and send you my comments.
I am very busy in the next few days, so I won't be able to start till Monday if that's alright with you?

I should be able to finish it by the middle of next week.
I will send you Section 3 tomorrow night, and the other sections over the weekend.

Making positive comments

First of all I think you have done a great job.
I have now had a chance to look at your manuscript, it looks very good.
I was really impressed with …
The only comments I have to make are:

Suggesting changes

While I like the idea of … I am not convinced that …
I'm not sure whether …
It might not be a bad idea to …
Have you thought about …?
It seems that …

Asking for clarification

I have a few questions to ask.
Could you just clarify a couple of aspects for me:

Replying with revised version attached

I have read the manuscript carefully and made several changes and corrections.
I hope I have not changed the sense of what you wanted to say.
Attached are my comments.
I think the paper still needs some work before sending to the journal.
Please keep me up to date on the progress of this manuscript.
Let me know if you need any more help.
Please give me a call if I can be of any help.
Don't hesitate to contact me if you need any more help.
I hope this helps.

Replying to comments

Bogdan, you did a great job, thanks so much!
Thank you for your comments—they were really useful.
I completely understand what you mean when you say … Thanks for bringing it up.
Many thanks for this. All points noted.
Yes, I see what you mean.
Thanks your comments were really helpful.

14.17   Referees reports

Making a summary of the paper

The paper deals with ...
The paper gives a good description of ...
This manuscript reports some results on the use of ...
The aim is to assess the quality of ...
This paper has many positive aspects ...

General criticisms

This paper aims to report the analysis of ... yet the author writes ...
The author needs to clarify the following points ...
Despite the title of the paper, I believe that the paper does not deal with X at all. Specifically ...
The analysis in Section 2 only covers ... Even though these are important parameters, they do not ...
Although the description of X and the samples collected seems to be detailed, accurate, and well documented, the analytical work and the discussion on Y are in need of major revision.
The manuscript does not present any improvement on the analytical procedure already described in the literature; moreover the authors fail to ...
The discussion should be reviewed since it is mainly based on results published in ...

Specific comments

Abstract: What is the real advantage of the proposed procedure with respect to ...?
page 3 line 12: The word *definite* is misspelled.
page 4: Perhaps Figure 2 could be deleted.
The following information is missing in Section 2:
There seems to be a missing reference in the bibliography.

Recommending rejection

For the above reasons, I believe that the paper is not innovative enough to be published in ...
The paper is not suitable for publication in its present form, since it does not fit the minimum requirements of originality and significance in the field covered by the Journal.

14.18   Author's reply to referees and editors

Asking for extension to deadlines

I am writing to ask whether it would be possible to extend the deadline for final submission of our paper until June 14.

The referees asked for several new experiments which will take us an extra two or three weeks to perform.

I apologize for the inconvenience caused by its late submission.

I am writing to inform you that due to unforeseen circumstances, we have to withdraw our paper.

Enclosing revised manuscript and reply to referees' reports

Attached is the revised version of our paper.

As requested, we have prepared a revised version of our manuscript, which we hope addresses the issues raised by the two reviewers.

As requested, I'm sending you the paper with the changes tracked.

Saying how your reply to the referees is organized

Below are our responses to the reviewers. The reviewers' comments are in italics, and our responses are numbered.

Rather than going through each report individually, we have organized our response under general areas.

Making positive comments about the reviewer's comments

Please extend my sincere thanks to the paper reviewers for their helpful comments.

The reviewer's suggestion is certainly helpful and …

The reviewer is right.

These two comments made us realize that …

Outlining changes made

We have improved the paper along the lines suggested by the Referees.

I have considered all the comments and suggestions made by reviewers of this paper, and I have incorporated most of them in the final version of this paper.

We have amended the paper addressing most of the comments provided in the referees' reports.

The tables have been enlarged and we hope they are now clearer.

The Abstract and the first sections have been improved.

We have amended the paper following the indications that you and the referees gave us.

There is now a new table (Table 1) reporting the ...

We have reduced the abstract to 150 words.

On the basis of Ref 1's first comment, we changed several parts which, as you can see, have been tracked.

Saying why some changes were not made

Reviewer 1 raised some substantial criticisms that would entail an almost completely new version of the paper.

We have tried to address the points he made but we have not been able to completely put into action all the recommendations he suggested. In order to do that, we would have gone beyond the intended scope of our paper.

Actually, this is not entirely true. In fact, ...

I understand what the referee means, however ...

The referee is absolutely right when he says .. Yet, ...

Concluding

Overall we hope we have addressed the main points raised by the reviewers.

Once again we would like to thank the reviewers for their very useful input and we also found your summary most helpful.

14.19   Generic problems

Describing

Unfortunately I have a problem with your ...

There seems to be a problem with ...

I'm afraid there is a slight problem.

I am not sure I can ...

That might cause us ...

I think the server may not be working correctly.

I am not sure whether you sent me the right file.

Trying to understand the problem

I am not completely clear what the problem is.
I'm sorry but I don't seem to be able to understand the problem. If possible could you give me more details to clarify the situation.
I'm not really clear about this—please clarify.
So if I have understood correctly, the problem is ...
So you are saying that ...

Showing that you have understood

Right, I understand.
OK that's clear now.
OK I am clear now.
Fine.

Resolving

OK. I'll see what I can do.
I'm sorry about that. I will look into it immediately.
Don't worry I am sure we can sort it out.
I'll look into it and get back to you first thing tomorrow morning.
I will contact you again shortly.
Let me know if there is anything else I can do for you.
Just give me a call if you need anything else.

Saying that the problem is being resolved

I promise I'll have it back to you by the end of this week.
Rest assured that you'll have it within the next two days.
I'll do it as a matter of urgency.
I'll make it my top priority.
I'm just writing to assure you that we are working on the problem.

Explaining the cause of the problem

The reason why this happened is ...
This was due to ...
It was related to ...

14.20 Asking for and giving clarification

Asking for clarification when you don't understand

I'm not sure what you mean by …
What exactly do you mean by …?
Sorry, what's a "xxx"?

Giving clarification when reader didn't understand

What I meant by xxx is …
My point is that …
In other words …
So what I'm saying is …
So what I am asking is …
So my question is …
In other words …

Giving clarification when recipient thought they understood but hadn't

Sorry, no what I meant was …
Sorry about the confusion, what I actually meant was …
Sorry I obviously didn't make myself clear.

Checking that you've understood

I'm assuming you mean …
Do you mean that …?
So are you saying that …?
By xxx do you mean …?

Checking whether recipient may have misunderstood

I am a bit concerned that you may have misinterpreted my email.
You sounded a little annoyed in your last mail. Maybe I had not expressed myself properly.

Acknowledging misunderstanding

OK, I'm sorry—you are right. I misunderstood.
Sorry about that, we obviously had our wires crossed!
Sorry for the confusion.

Hoping you have been clear

I hope this helps clarify the problems.
Does this all make sense now?
Have I clarified everything for you?
Do you understand what I mean now?

Replying when you have been given clarification

OK, understood.
OK, I'm clear now.
OK, but I'm still not clear about …

14.21 Thanking

Thanking recipient for responding to your email

Many thanks for your email.
Thanks for getting back to me.
Thank you for the quick response.

Thanking in advance

Thanks in advance.
Thanks for any help you can give me.
Thank you very much for your assistance.
I thank you in advance for your cooperation.

Thanking for help already given

Thanks for your help in this matter.
Thank you for your help in solving this problem.
Many thanks for this.
Thanks once again for all your trouble.

14.22 Apologizing

For not answering mail sooner

Sorry for the delay in getting back to you.
Sorry I haven't replied sooner.
I apologize for not sending you the information you requested.
Apologies for the late reply.
Please accept our apologies for not getting back to you sooner.

For not answering mail sooner: excuses

Please accept my apologies, I was convinced that I had replied to you.
Sorry, but I have only just read your message now.
I have just got back from a conference.
I've been away for the last few days.
Sorry, but our server has been down, so we haven't been receiving any mails.
Sorry but we've been having emailing problems.
Sorry but your email must have gone into the spam.

For your email not arriving

For some reason my last email had delivery problems. So here it is again just in case you didn't get it first time round.
Please reply to the above address as our regular connection is down. Thanks very much.

For sending an incomplete email

Sorry I accidentally hit the send button.

Repeating apology at end of mail

Again sorry for the delay.
Once again, apologies for any trouble this may have caused you.
Thanks and once again sorry for not getting back to you straight away.

14.23   Sending attachments

Telling receiver about your mail

I'm attaching …
Please find attached …
Attached you will find …
Here is …
As you will see from the attached copy …

Asking for confirmation of receipt

Please confirm / acknowledge receipt.
Let me know if you have received it.
I'd appreciate it if you could confirm your receipt via either fax or email.
Please could you acknowledge receipt of this mail as I am not sure we have your correct address.
Let me know if you can't open the file.

Giving confirmation

This is just to confirm that I received your attachment. I will get back to you by 9.00 tomorrow morning.
I confirm receipt of your attachment.

Telling sender you couldn't read the mails / attachments

Sorry I couldn't read your mail—it just has a series of strange characters.
I received your mail, but I'm afraid I can't open the attachment.
When I try to open the file the system crashes.

Telling sender they forgot to send the attachment

Thanks for your mail but I'm afraid you forgot to send the attachment.
I think you forgot to send the attachment.
I can't find the attachment.

Sending attachment again

Sorry, I just sent you an email without the attachments.
Sorry about the problems. Here's the attachment again. Let me know if you can read it.
Oops. Sorry. Here it is.

14.24　Technical problems with email

Problems with Internet connection

Sorry our server has been down all morning.
Sorry but they are doing maintenance work tomorrow morning and I won't have access to my email.
My Internet service is currently not working at home, which also means I can't call out. But I should still be able to receive incoming phone calls.

14.25　Out of office message

Adrian Wallwork is on leave from Monday 07/08 to Wed 16/08. If you have any problems or queries please contact Anna Southern at anna.southern@virgilio.it.
I'm out of the office all day today but will get back to you tomorrow regarding any urgent messages.
If you have any urgent messages you can contact me on my mobile: [0039] 347 …

Chapter 15

Tense Usage

15.1 What's the buzz?

Choose the correct form.

1. Please find enclosed our final manuscript. We *1) have addressed / addressed* all the comments that the reviewer *2) has made / made*. In fact, we *3) have added / added* a new section on Y. However, we *4) are / do* not agree with the referee's comment on the appendix. We *5) have decided / decided* to leave the appendix, as we believe it *6) will help / helps* the reader to do X. If you *7) require / will require* any further explanations, please ...

2. You may remember that we *8) met / have met* at the conference on X. You *9) mentioned / have mentioned* that there might be a possibility of working in your lab for X, one of our PhD students who *10) is graduated / has a degree* in K. She *11) has carried / been carrying* out research into Y but *12) is now studying / now studies* Z. In fact for the last three months, she *13) is investigating / has been investigating* Z1. She *14) is / would be* interested in continuing this research with your team as you *15) have gained / have been gaining* considerable experience in this field. If a stage in your lab *16) is / will be* possible, I *17) will / would* be extremely grateful if you *18) can / could* let me know by the end of next month since ...

3. Last week I *19) have attended / attended* the X workshop on Y. I *20) have found / found* your presentation on Z very interesting. I *21) was wondering / wondered* whether you *22) have / had* a paper on this topic. If so I *23) would appreciate / appreciated* it if you *24) would send / sent* me a copy to the following address.

4. We *25) like / would like* to submit for publication in X our paper entitled "Y". This paper is an extended version of an abstract which *26) has been / was* published in the proceedings of Z. We *27) have also added / also added* some new results which we believe *28) are / will* be of interest to the scientific community. We *29) look / are looking* forward to hearing from you.

For more similar exercises see Chapter 27 in *English for Academic Research: Grammar Exercises.*

****

© Springer International Publishing Switzerland 2016
A. Wallwork, *English for Academic Correspondence*,
English for Academic Research, DOI 10.1007/978-3-319-26435-6_15

This chapter only contains those tenses, forms, and modal verbs that are most frequently used in emails and letters. I have tried to explain the subtle differences between the tenses as well as the possible dangers of misusing them.

The mini grammar in this chapter outlines how to:

- use the most common tenses in English

- differentiate the subtle shades of meaning between one tense and another

- avoid ambiguity and misunderstandings in misusage of tenses

- distinguish between various modal verbs

- put words in the correct order

- link sentences together

If you wish to improve your grammar you will find the following books of help:

English for Academic Research: Grammar, Usage and Style

English for Academic Research: Grammar Exercises

English for Academic Research: Vocabulary Exercises

English for Academic Research: Writing Exercises

KEY TO EXERCISE 1) have addressed 2) made (has made) 3) have added 4) do 5) decided 6) will help / helps 7) require 8) met 9) mentioned 10) has a degree 11) has carried 12) is now studying 13) has been investigating 14) is / would be 15) have 16) is 17) would 18) could 19) attended 20) found 21) was wondering 22) have 23) would 24) would send 25) would like 26) was (has been) 27) have also added 28) will 29) look

15.2 Use of the present simple

Use the present simple:

To describe states and situations that don't change.

The earth *revolves* around the sun.

The journal only *accepts* manuscripts in English.

Where *are* you from? I *come* from Ethiopia.

To talk about habits and things that are done regularly.

> What *do you do*? I *study* mathematics at the University of Prague.

> How often *do you go* to conferences? I *go* about twice a year.

To give a feeling of distance in formal emails, with the verbs indicated in the examples below.

> I *write* to complain about the poor service I received at your hotel.

> I *trust* you are keeping well.

> We *wish* to inform you that …

> We *advise* you that the deadline for the manuscript expired last week.

> I *regret* that we will not be able to meet your deadline.

> I *appreciate* the fact / I *realize* that you must be very busy, but …

> I *acknowledge* / *confirm* receipt of your paper.

> I *look forward* to hearing from you in the near future.

To describe to referees how the manuscript looks now compared to the original version.

> Figure 3 now *appears* in the Appendix.

> Table 6 now *contains* data on …

> The Abstract *is* now considerably shorter.

To report what others have told us.

> Professor Kamatachi *sends* her kindest regards.

> Kai *says* hello.

Note: Certain verbs are generally only used in the present simple rather than the present continuous (see 15.4). So, even if you are talking about something that is taking place now, you still need to use the present simple (both face to face and in emails). The present simple in such cases can be used in both formal and informal situations.

> *Do you agree* with what I am saying? Yes, I *agree*.

> I *assure* you / I *guarantee* / I *promise* I will be on time.

> I *imagine* you must have had a long journey to get here.

> I *notice* from your badge that you are from the university of …

> I *hear* / *understand* / *gather* that you are doing a presentation this afternoon.

15.3 Non-use of the present simple

Do <u>not</u> use the present simple:

To make suggestions, ask for advice, or offer to do things. Use *shall* or *will* instead.

Shall I email you to confirm the arrangements?

Shall we go on the trip tomorrow?

Shall I open the window?

I will let you know the results of the tests tomorrow.

To react to suggestions made in an email or face to face that you are now responding to. Instead, use *will* (see 15.5).

Sender: Please can you tell Prof Davis to contact me. Response: OK, I *will let* him now.

Sender: If possible, could do this by Friday? Response: *I'll do* my best.

Questioner: What would you like to drink? Response: *I'll have* a beer.

To talk about actions or situations that began in the past and continue into the present. Use the present perfect instead (see 15.9).

I *have lived* here for six months. [Not: I live here for six months]

15.4 Use of the present continuous

Use the present continuous:

To describe an incomplete action that is going on now at this moment.

What *is he saying*? I don't understand.

What *are you doing*? *I'm just downloading* some photos to show you.

To talk about an incomplete action that is going on during this period of time, or a trend.

I *am working* on a new project with Dr Huria.

The number of people using Facebook *is growing* steadily.

To talk about a temporary event or situation.

> I usually teach at the university, but this month I *am doing* seminars at another institute.

> I have only just arrived so I *am staying* in university accommodation until I find something of my own.

To give a more friendly tone in emails and letters, particularly with verbs such as *write, enclose, attach, look forward to.*

> I *am writing* to let you know that the paper has finally been accepted.

> I *am attaching* those photos that I took at the social dinner

> I *am really looking forward* to seeing you again.

To talk about future programmed arrangements. In the question form, it does not matter whether or not you know that your interlocutor has made plans or not.

> I *am seeing* Chandra on Monday [Chandra and I have already arranged this].

> *We're flying* there on Monday. [We've already bought our plane ticket].

> What *are you doing* this weekend? *We're going* skiing.

> When *are you leaving*? I *am leaving* after my presentation this afternoon.

15.5   Non-use of continuous forms

The types of verb below are not generally used in the continuous form (i.e., present continuous, past continuous, present perfect continuous). They describe states rather than actions.

Verbs of opinion and mental state: for example, *believe, forget, gather, imagine, know, mean, notice, recognize, remember, think* (i.e., have an opinion), *understand*

> I *gather* you have been having some problems with the software.

Verbs of senses and perception: *feel, hear, see, seem, look, smell, taste*

> This fish *tastes* delicious.

Verbs that express emotions and desires: for example, *hate, hope, like, love, prefer, regret, want, wish*

> *Do you want* anymore wine?

> *I wish* my wife was here, she would love this place.

Verbs of measurement: for example, *contain, cost, hold, measure, weigh*

> This table *contains* the data on xyz.

> The recipient *holds* up to six liters.

When the above verbs refer to actions rather than states, they may be used in the continuous form. Examples:

> We *are having* dinner with the team tonight. [*have* means "eat" not "possess"]

> We *were thinking* about contacting them for a collaboration. [*think* means "consider" not "have an opinion"]

15.6   Future simple [*will*]

Use *will*:

To give a response in an email to a request by the sender. The recipient uses *will* to say what he / she plans to do to meet the request.

> Sender: Could you have a look at the doc and tell me what you think of it.

> Recipient: OK, *I'll do* it tomorrow morning.

> Sender: I was wondering whether you might be able to give me a hand with my presentation.

> Recipient: OK, *I'll have* a look at my diary when I get to the office and *I'll let* you know when will be a good time for me.

> *I'll contact* Dr Njimi and ask her to mail you.

> *I'll be* in touch soon.

To respond to a situation that presents itself at that moment.

> My mobile's ringing. *I'll just have to* answer it.

> Person A: I am having problems with this translation. Person B: *I'll help you* with it if you like.

Person A: I don't really understand. Person B: *I'll try* to explain myself better. *I'll give* you an example.

Person A: Would you like something to eat? Person B: No, *I'll have* something later thank you.

To refer to attachments or enclosures.

As you *will see* from the attached copy …

Below you *will find* the responses to your points re ..

Herein you *will find* enclosed two copies of the contract.

To predict future events, based on personal intuitions.

The number of congresses *will go* down if large-screen videoconferencing becomes possible.

I'm pretty sure Qatar *won't win* the World Cup.

To talk about future states and events with verbs that don't take the present continuous (see 15.4)

We *will know* tomorrow.

She *will be* 50 next week.

To indicate formal events

The university *will celebrate* its 500th anniversary next year.

The next edition of the conference *will be held* in Karachi.

The seminar *will take place* at 10.00 in Room 6.

To make requests.

Will you give me a hand with this translation please?

Will you let me know how you get on?

15.7 Future continuous

Use the future continuous:

To give the idea that something will happen irrespectively of your own intentions or wishes. There is a sense of inevitability—the future continuous implies that something is beyond your control.

> I'm sorry but I *won't be attending* your presentation tomorrow. [This gives the idea that the decision does not depend on you but unfortunately there are more urgent tasks that require your intention]

> *I'll be going* to the station myself so I can give you a lift there if you like. [This gives the idea that I am not doing you a personal favor by taking you to the station, as in any case I have to go there myself; it is slightly more polite than saying "I am going to the station"]

> Person A: Would you like to come with us to dinner tonight? Person B: I'm very sorry but I *will be going* with Professor Chowdry's group. [I have no choice in the matter, I have to join Chowdry's group]

In all of the above cases the use of the future simple [will] would give a very different impression. In the first example, if you say "I won't attend" it gives the idea that you do not want to attend. In the second example, "I will go" means that you make the decision now as a personal favor for your interlocutor. In the third example, "I will go" means that you spontaneously decide to go with Chowdry's group because you don't want to go with Person A.

This sense of politeness is also found with the past continuous, for example:

> I *wonder* whether you might be able to help me.

> I *was wondering* whether you might be able to me.

The past continuous is a more tentative form and thus more polite.

The future continuous is also used in the following cases too:

To talk about plans and arrangements, again when you want to give the sense that your actions do not strictly depend on you. The implication is that this is simply the way things are.

> I *will be paying* by credit card.

> My boss *will be arriving* on the 10 o'clock flight.

> As of 15 January we *will be increasing* the cost of subscription by 6%.

> We hereby inform you that from September 1 our institute *will be moving* to the address indicated below.

To give the idea that you have already been working to make something happen.

I *will send* you the paper next week. [This sounds like you made the decision now as a reaction to your interlocutor's request]

I *will be sending* you the paper next week. [This sounds like you had already made the decision independently of the current request by your interlocutor]

To describe some action that will be underway at a certain point in the future. In this sense it is the future equivalent to the present continuous and past continuous.

When I get to Manchester it *will probably be raining*. [i.e., it will probably have already started to rain].

This time next year I *will be working* in Professor Jamani's lab and *I will finally be earning* some money!

15.8   *be going to*

Use *be going to* plus the infinitive:

To refer to plans and intentions that you have already made decisions about, but for which you have not necessarily made the final arrangements:

She's going to try and get an internship somewhere. [This is her plan but she hasn't necessarily started to look yet]

Are you going to see the Sagrada Familia while you're in Barcelona? [Is this part of your planned itinerary?]

To refer to plans that indicate solitary activities that do not involve making arrangements with other people.

After the presentation I *am going to* have a long bath back at the hotel.

Tonight I *am just going to* read through my notes, then I *am going to* go to bed.

To make predictions based on present or past evidence. In some cases the evidence is already there that something is starting to happen.

Look at the sky—it looks like it *is going to* snow. [The cloud formation is such that snow can be expected]

It *is going to be* tough for students with the cuts in education that the government is planning to introduce. [Past experience shows that when spending is cut, students have difficulty paying their fees]

15.9 Past simple

Use the simple past:

To talk about completed actions in the recent past (even one second ago) or the distant past.

> I *sent* the mail below to them on October 22, but have heard nothing since.

> Professor Putin *called* this morning to verify ...

> The University of Bologna is the oldest university in the world it *was founded* in 1088.

Even if the precise moment is not mentioned, but this moment will be clear to the recipient, use the simple past.

> Regarding the data you asked for, I *forgot* to mention in my previous mail that ...

> Please find attached the market report I *promised* you.

15.10 Present perfect simple

The present perfect often connects the past to the present. The action took place in the past but is not explicitly specified because we are more interested in the result than in the action itself.

Use the present perfect:

To indicate actions that took place during a period that has not yet finished.

> *I've written* more than 10 papers on the topic. [And I will probably publish more research on this topic]

> So far I *have responded* to two out of three of the referee's reports. [I still have time to reply to the third referee]

Compare:

> *Did you receive* my last email message sent on 10 March? [Precise date given]

> I just wanted to check whether you *have received* any news from Professor Shankar. [I don't know if you have received news yet]

To talk about actions took place at an indefinite or unknown time.

> I *have been* to six conferences on this subject.

> I *have been informed* that …

> I'm sorry I *haven't replied* earlier but I *have been* out of the office all week.

To talk about actions or states that began in the past and continue into the present.

> I *have worked* for here six months. [NB Not: I work here for six months].

> We *have not made* much progress in this project so far.

Note: When talking about an action's duration use *for* if you talk about the period of time. Use *since* when you say when the action began. Examples:

> for five years, for a long time, for more than an hour

> since 2011, since January, since he joined our research team

To specify what is new and to indicate what actions have been taken.

> This is to inform you that my email address *has changed*. From now on please use:

> I *have spoken* to our administration department and they *have forwarded* your request to the head of department.

> I *have looked* at your revisions and *have just added* a few comments. Hope they help.

> A new figure *has been inserted* in Section 2.

> We *have reduced* the length of the Abstract, as suggested by Reviewer 2.

> We *have not made* any changes to Table 1 because we think that …

To say *it's the first / second time* that something happened. Note: Do not use the present simple in such cases.

> This is the first time I *have done* a presentation—I am very nervous.

> This is the second time I *have been* to Caracas.

Do <u>not</u> use the present perfect to talk or ask about the details of the action, use the simple past. Compare:

> *I've seen her present* twice before so I don't want to watch her again. [The consequence is more important than the precise moment when I saw her presentation]

> *Did you see* her at the last conference or the one before? [I am now referring to a specific moment].

> *Have you ever bought* anything from Amazon?

> What exactly *did you buy*? How long *did it take* to receive them?

15.11 Present perfect continuous

Use the present perfect continuous:

To describe actions and trends that started in the past and continue in the present.

How long *have you been working* in the field of psycholinguistics?

I've been going to presentations all morning, I'm really tired.

To talk about the effect of recent events.

Why are you covered in ink? *I've been repairing* the photocopier.

He's been working for 14 hours nonstop that's why he looks so tired.

To outline problems or to introduce a topic in emails and on the telephone.

I gather you *have been experiencing* problems in downloading the conference program.

I've been talking to Jim about the fault in your computer but I can't find your email describing ...

15.12 Non-use of present perfect continuous

Do not use the present perfect continuous for completed actions or when you talk about the number of occasions that something has happened or when you specify a quantity [except in days, hours, minutes, etc.]. Use the present perfect simple or past simple instead. Compare:

We *have been writing* a lot of papers recently. [And we are likely to write some more].

We *have written* six papers in the last three years. [The next paper will be the seventh; the action of writing the first six papers is over]

I *have worked* on several projects in this field. [These several projects are now finished, but I am likely to work on similar projects in the future]

I *have been working* for three years on this project. [This project is still ongoing]

I *worked* on three projects in that field, before switching to a completely new line of research. [I now work in a different area]

He's been talking on the phone all morning. [And he is still talking now].

I've talked to him and we've resolved the matter. [The discussion is over]

Note the difference between the simple past, the present perfect, and the present perfect continuous:

I *have been trying* to call you. [And I will probably continue calling you]

I *have tried* to call you. [Probably recently, but I've stopped trying]

I *tried* to call you. [At a specific moment, for example, this morning, yesterday, at the weekend, I will not try again]

15.13   The imperative form

Use the imperative:

To tell people what you want them to do, but without seeming impolite. In any case, particularly in emails, you can make the sentence more polite and soft if you use *please*. NB there is no comma after *please*.

Let me know if you have any problems.

Say hello to Cindy for me.

Please *find* attached a copy of my paper.

Please *do not hesitate* to contact me if you need any further clarifications.

To wish people well.

Have a great day.

Enjoy your meal.

Have a nice weekend.

Have a great Thanksgiving!

Happy Easter to everyone.

A Happy Christmas to you all.

If you wish to be more formal you can say:

I would like to take this opportunity to wish you a peaceful and prosperous New Year.

15.14 Zero and first conditional forms

The zero conditional [if + present + present] expresses general truths and scientific facts. It means "every time that" or "whenever".

> If you *mix* green and red you *get* brown.

> If you *work* in industry you generally *get* paid more than if you work in research.

The first conditional [if + present + will] is used to talk about real future situations, rather than general truths that are always valid.

> We wish to inform you that if we *do not receive* the revised manuscript by the end of this month, we *will be forced* to withdraw your contribution from the special issue.

> I *will go* on the trip tomorrow if it *doesn't* rain.

15.15 Second conditional

The second conditional [if + past simple + would] is used to refer to improbable or unreal future situations, or when making cautious requests.

> If I *had* enough money I *would* probably retire. [At the moment I don't have enough money]

> If my department *gave* me the funding, I *would* do my research abroad. [My department is unlikely to fund me]

> If I *were* you, I *would reduce* the number of slides in your presentation. [I am not you]

> *Would it be* OK with you, if I *delayed* sending you the revisions until next week? [I am making a cautious request]

> *Would you mind* if we *met* in the conference bar rather than at your hotel?

> If we *took* a taxi, it *would be* much quicker.

Note: Some people, particularly in the USA, use *would* in both halves of the sentence.

In replies to referees reports, the second conditional may be used to indicate the effort involved to fulfill the referee's requirements:

> If we *did* as Ref. 1 suggests, this *would* entail doing several more experiments which *would* take at least six months work.

> If we *removed* Figure 3, the reader *might / would not be able* to understand the significance of our data.

There is a particular form of conditional that is used almost exclusively in emails and business letters, which is when *would* [or *could*] is used in both parts of the sentence. This construction represents a form of courtesy.

> I *would be* grateful if you *would send* me a copy of your paper.

> If you *could get this* to me before the end of today it *would be* great.

> Any information you *could give* us *would be* very much appreciated.

> I *would very much appreciate* it if you *could get back* to me within the next few days.

Would is also used in polite requests:

> I *would like* to inform you that ..

> I *would like* to take this opportunity to …

15.16   Third conditional

The third conditional [if + past perfect + would have + past participle] expresses how things might have been if something had (not) happened. It can be used to express regrets and hypotheses about the past, missed opportunities, and criticisms of oneself or others.

> If I *had realized* how long it would take me to prepare the presentation, I *would never have offered* to do it.

> I *would have come* to the airport to meet you if I *had known* that you were coming.

In conditional phrases you can change the order of the *if* clause and the main clause.

> I *will help* you if you *want*. / If you *want* I *will help* you.

> If I *had* the opportunity I *would* get a job in industry. / I *would* get a job in industry, if I *had* the opportunity

You can also mix the forms.

> If I *had not met* Professor Rossi, I *would not be* in Italy now.

15.17 Modal verbs expressing ability and possibility: *can, could, may, might*

Use *can* and *cannot* to express a general ability to do (or not be able to do) something whenever you want.

> I *can* use many different programming languages.

> I am afraid I *can't* speak English very well.

Use *can* to express certain 100% possibility and *cannot* 100% impossibility, *may [not]* for 50%.

> I *can* let you know tomorrow. [I am certain that I will be able to let you know tomorrow]

> We *cannot* cut the paper any further without losing much of the significance. [It would be impossible to make further cuts]

> I am afraid that I *cannot* attend your seminar. [It is impossible for me to come]

> I *may* go to at least one of the social events, but I am not sure I will have time. [Perhaps I will go]

You can also use *may*, *might*, and *could* to speculate about the future or talk about probability.

> You *may* remember we met last year at the EFX conference in Barcelona.

> We *may* have to abandon the project.

> They *may* not get the funding if the government keeps making cuts in education.

> Please accept our apologies for any inconvenience this *may* have caused you.

> I *could* be wrong. [But not necessarily]

> The results they obtained *could* / *might* be misleading [I am speculating]

15.18 Modal verbs expressing advice and obligation: *have to*, *must*, *need*, *should*

When you advise someone what to do use *should*. Alternatively, use *must* if you want to give them a very strong recommendation.

You *should* try getting in touch with her via Facebook.

You *must* go and see the cathedral while you're here—it is so beautiful.

Use *should* when some kind of moral or ethical issue is involved, or when you think something is likely to happen or would be a good idea.

The government *should* spend more on research.

I think they *should* avoid having too many parallel sessions at conferences.

We *should* try and get to the museum early to avoid the queues.

I sent it via DHL yesterday so you *should* get it by tomorrow at the latest.

At the end of an email *should* is often used to tell the recipient that they are free to ask further questions, etc. Note that *should* comes before the subject.

Should you have any questions, please let us know.

Should you need any further clarifications, do not hesitate to contact me.

Use *have to* when you talk about responsibilities (i.e., to show that an obligation probably comes from some other person, not from you). If something is not necessary or is not your responsibility, use *don't have to* or *don't need to*.

In my country you only *have to* wear seatbelts if you are driving on a motorway.

I *have to* catch the 6.30 train to be at work on time.

You *have to* take your shoes off when you go in the mosque.

At my institute you *don't necessarily have to* always work in the lab, you can work from home if you want.

You *don't have to* send it via fax, you can email it if you like.

Use *must* when you are making a deduction based on present circumstances.

It appears that some mistake *must* have been made.

Could you send your fax number again as I think I *must* have the wrong number.

I realize you *must* be very busy at the moment but if you could spare a moment I would be most grateful.

Avoid *have to* and *must* when you are giving instructions, just use the imperative.

To get there, just *go* out of the lobby and *turn* right, then *go* straight on for 100 meters.

Please let me know how you *get* on.

However, if you are an authority (e.g., a conference organizer, editor of a journal), then you can use *must* in a formal situation in order to outline a procedure.

Applications *must* be received by 30 June.

Papers *must* be sent in both pdf and Word formats.

The software *must* be dispatched by courier.

If you want to talk about a past obligation, the form you use will depend on whether you fulfilled the obligation or not.

Yesterday I *had to* give a presentation—I was very nervous. [Obligation fulfilled]

I *was supposed* to do a presentation, but in the end my prof did it for me. [Obligation not fulfilled]

I *didn't have to* do a presentation, they let me do a poster session instead. [Potential obligation turned out not to be necessary]

I *was going to* do a presentation, but then I decided it would be too much work. [Unfulfilled intention]

15.19 Modal verbs for offers, requests, invitations, and suggestions: *can*, *may*, *could*, *would*, *shall*, *will*

Use *can*, *may*, and *shall* to offer to do something. *May* is more formal.

> *May / Can / Shall* I help you?

Use *can*, *could*, *will*, and *would* to request something. *Could* and *would* are more polite.

> *Can / Could / Will / Would* you help me?

Use *would you like* to invite someone.

> *Would you like* to come out for dinner tonight?

Use *shall* to make a suggestion.

> *Shall* I open the window?

> *Shall* we go to the bar?

In emails *can* and *could* are often used to make polite requests. In that sense, they are not really questions, so many native speakers do not put a question mark at the end of the sentence.

> *Could* you send me the doc as soon as you have a moment. Thanks.

> *Can* you give me your feedback by the end of the week. Thanks.

You can make your request softer by preceding *could* with *do you think*. In such cases the recipient is given more chance to say "no".

> *Could* you translate the attached document for me.

> *Do you think you could* translate the attached document for me?

You can also make it more polite by using *please*.

> *Please could* you tell me who I should contact regarding registering for the conference.

Questions marks are used when there is a real question, that is, when you are expecting an answer.

> *Can* we meet up some time next week?

> By the way, *can* you speak Spanish?

No questions marks are used with *may* in the following types of situations.

May I wish you a very happy new year.

May I take this opportunity to ...

May I remind you that ...

15.20   Word order

SUBJECT + VERB + OBJECT

The standard word order in English is: (1) subject, (2) verb, (3) direct object, (4) indirect object

I am attaching a file.

We are meeting at the bar at six o'clock.

If there are two objects and one is a pronoun, with verbs like *send*, *give*, *email*, *forward*, and *write*, there are two possible orders:

Please forward this message to her / Please forward her this message

But in other cases, that is, with two nouns, the direct object usually comes first:

Please send my regards to Professor Smith.

Did you send the attachment in your last email?

INVERSION OF SUBJECT AND MAIN VERB/AUXILIARY VERB

Note the inversions (highlighted in italics) of the normal word order in these cases:

• In questions and requests.

Are you sure?

Have you done it yet?

Can you help me?

Will you let me know how you want me to proceed—thanks.

If possible, *could you* do this before tomorrow.

- After *so* and *neither / nor*.

  I am afraid I don't have any clear data yet, *nor do I* expect to have any before the end of the month.

  I expect to be able to meet the deadline and *so does* my co-author.

- In sentences that begin with *only* or a negation.

  Only when / Not until we receive these corrections, *will we* be able to proceed with the publication.

- After *should* in formal expressions.

  Should you need any further clarifications, please do not hesitate to contact me.

ADJECTIVES

Adjectives are normally placed before the nouns that they describe:

  We hope we will be able to find a satisfactory solution.

If there are a lot of adjectives, use this order: quantity, size, color, origin, material, use.

  A large white Russian plastic bag.

  The department is offering ten 3-year full-time contracts.

If you put an adjective or description after the noun, then you need to use a relative clause, that is, a phrase that begins with *who*, *that*, or *which*.

  I sent the paper, which had been revised by the proofreader, to the editor.

PAST PARTICIPLES

Most past participles can be placed after the noun they refer to, although some can come before or after. I suggest that you always place them after, then you are less likely to make a mistake.

  The results obtained prove that...

  The method described is ...

ADVERBS

Adverbs of frequency and *also*, *only*, and *just* go after (i) *am / is / are / was / were* (ii) between the subject and the verb, and (iii) between the auxiliary and the main verb.

(i)	I am *occasionally* late with deadlines.	I am *also* an expert chemist.
(ii)	I *sometimes* arrive late for work.	I *only* speak English and German.
(iii)	I have *often* given presentations.	I have *just* seen her presentation.

Adverbs of manner go at the end of the phrase.

She speaks English *quickly / fluently*.

Adverbs that indicate times of the day, week, year, etc. can always be located at the end of the sentence.

I can send you the package by courier *today / tomorrow morning / at 09.00*.

Note the position of *above*:

As mentioned *above*, this method only works if…

The *above*-mentioned method only works if…

LINK WORDS

Most link words can go either at the beginning or in the middle of the sentence.

We have lost most of our government funding. *As a result*, we will have to make some drastic cuts.

The paper was presented at an international conference. *In addition*, it is going to be published in…

I will, *however*, still require another two months to finish the work.

I have *thus* decided to withdraw my paper.

too and *as well* are generally found at the end of the sentence.

She has a degree in Physics and a Master's in analytical chemistry *too / as well*.

although, *though*, and *even though* can be placed in two positions.

Although he has worked here for years, he has never been given a contract.

He has never been given a contract *even though* he has worked here for years.

15.21 Link words

Below are some words that you can use to structure the content of your emails, letters and proposals; the first line of examples contains words that are perhaps a little less formal than the examples in the second line.

For an explanation of the difference in meaning between these words and phrases, see Chapter 13 of *English for Research: Grammar, Usage and Style.*

ORDERING AND SEQUENCING

first, then, next, at the same time, finally, in the end

firstly, secondly, simultaneously, subsequently, lastly

ADDING INFORMATION AND/OR MARKING A CHANGE IN TOPIC

another thing, while I'm at it, by the way, and, also

moreover, in addition, furthermore

DRAWING ATTENTION

note that, what is really important to note is

NB, please note that

CONTRASTING

although, though, even though, however, instead, on the other hand, even so

despite this, by contrast, nevertheless, on the contrary, nonetheless, conversely

CORRECTING OR GIVING DIFFERENT EMPHASIS TO PREVIOUS STATEMENT

actually, in fact

as a matter of fact, in reality

GIVING A PARALLEL

in the same way, similarly

by the same token, likewise, equally

GIVING EXAMPLES AND SPECIFYING

e.g., i.e., such as, like, this means that, in other words

for example, for instance, that is to say

INDICATING A RESULT

so

consequently, as a result therefore, thus, hence, thereby, accordingly

CONCLUDING

in sum

to conclude, in conclusion, in summary

Acknowledgments

Thanks to the following experts: Stewart Alsop (alsop-louie.com) and Susan Barnes, Chandler Davis, Andy Hunt (pragprog.com), Ibrahima Diagne, Jacquie Dutcher, Sue Fraser, Patrick Forsyth, Keith Harding, Susan Herring, Tarun Huria, Alex Lamb (www.alexlambtraining.com/index.html), Luciano Lenzini, Brian Martin, David Morand, Janice Nadler, Anna Southern, Richard Wiseman (http://richardwiseman.wordpress.com/tag/quirkology/), Mark Worden, Zheng Ting.

Massive thanks to Rogier A. Kievit and his 'Shit My Reviewers Say' website - keep up the good work!

I would like to thank the following researchers who provided me with emails and referees' reports for this book. Also big thanks to all my PhD students who over the last 10 years have given me a constant supply of typical academic emails.

Nicola Aloia, Michele Barbera, Bernadette Batteaux, Stefania Biagioni, Silvia Brambilla, Emilia Bramanti, Francesca Bretzel, Davide Castagnetti, Elena Castanas, Shourov Keith Chatterji, Patrizia Cioni, MariaPerla Colombini, Francesca Di Donato, Marco Endrizzi, Fabrizio Falchi, Roger Fuoco, Edi Gabellieri, Valeria Galanti, Silvia Gonzali, Tarun Huria, Kamatchi Ramasamy Chandra, Stefano Lenzi, Luciano Lenzini, Francesca Nicolini, Enzo Mingozzi, Elisabetta Morelli, Beatrice Pezzarossa, Marco Pardini, Roberto Pini, Emanuele Salerno, Daniel Sentenac, Paola Sgadò, Igor Spinella, Enzo Sparvoli, Pandey Sushil, Eliana Tassi, Elisabetta Tognoni, Eriko Tsuchida and Ting Zheng.

Special thanks to these people for providing materials for this new edition: Cian Blaix, Sofia Luzgina, Leonardo Magneschi, Maral Mahad, Bartolome Alles Salom, Shanshan Zhou.

Sources of the Factoids

Much of the information contained in the factoids is publicly available on the Internet. Below is more information about the sources for some of the factoids, quotations, and other statistics. The numbers in brackets indicate the number of the factoid, e.g. (2) = the second factoid or quotation.

Chapter 1

(2) based on a statistic that claims that more than 250 billion emails are sent every day (source: Wiki Answers): the total pile would be 25,000 kilometers high, it would weigh 1,250,000 metric tonnes, and all the printed emails would have a surface area of 15,592 square kilometers The cost in euros would be around one billion. (3) TNS "Digital Life" 10 Oct 2010.

Chapter 2

(1) personal communication; (2) Dr Tarun Huria, Indian Railways; (3)Dr Zheng Ting [aka Sophia Zheng], University of Shandong, Jinan, China. (4) www.theguardian.com/media/mind-your-language/2015/aug/24/hi-hey-hello-dear-reader-how-do-you-start-an-email

Chapter 3

(1,3,4) can be found in any book of quotations; (2) Fortune Magazine; (5) *Winning Sales Letters, John Fraser-Robinson*, David Grant Publishing, 2000

3.1 The statistic on people spending 40% of their time emailing comes from *I Hate People*, J Littman & M Hershon, published by Little, Brown and Company. I have been unable to locate the original source of the spell cheque poem in **13.4** (for the full version see http://www.greaterthings. com/Humor/Spelling_Chequer.htm), nor can I find the researchers involved in the Cambridge University inquiry into the phenomenal power of the human mind, which of course may be a total invention.

© Springer International Publishing Switzerland 2016
A. Wallwork, *English for Academic Correspondence*,
English for Academic Research, DOI 10.1007/978-3-319-26435-6

Chapter 4

The Observer 20 May 2001 based on research carried out by David Silver at the University of Washington; and Susan Herring at Indiana University.

Chapter 5

Info in the factoids all in the public domain.

5.11 *The Christopher Robin Birthday Book* by A.A. Milne, E.P. Dutton & Co. (1936).

Chapter 6

http://www.duboislc.org/ED-Watch/wordlist.html Note there are many sites and books listing the most common words. This one was intended to help teachers teach US schoolchildren to read and was taken from the book *The Reading Teacher's Book of Lists*, by Fry and Kress, John Wiley, 2006. It is thus considerably biased by the kinds of books found in the US curriculum (this explains the position of *Indian* at 283rd, where I imagine that *Indian* refers to native Americans, and probably indicates that the list may have been compiled several decades ago). I chose this list because it contained the most surprising items, and therefore I thought it would be good for discussion purposes. A more up to date list can be found at: https://en.wikipedia.org/wiki/Most_common_words_in_English.

Chapter 7

(1,2) Business Life, April 2008; (3) Fortune, March 2, 1998, (5) http://www.personneltoday.com/articles/2008/07/25/46874/lying-on-cvs-for-job-applications-rises-to-17.html; (6) http://money.guardian.co.uk/work/story/0,1456,1589620,00.html

Chapter 8

I hate people! J Littman and M Hershon, Little, Brown and Company, 2009.

Chapter 9

The original book of laws, called *Murphy's Law - And Other Reasons Why Things Go Wrong* was written by Arthur Bloch and published by Price/Stern/Sloan Publishers in 1977. But all these laws are now available on many websites.

Chapter 10

(2) Andrew Hunt, *Pragmatic Thinking and Learning: Refactor Your Wetware*, The Pragmatic Bookshelf, 2008 (3) Personal communication.

10.4 The structure was based on ideas from *Understanding Misunderstanding* by Nancy Slessenger, publ. Vine House Essential Ltd, 2003.

10.9 Quoted in *Business Communications*, Claudia Rawlins, HarperCollins Publishers, Inc, 1993.

Chapter 11

http://shitmyreviewerssay.tumblr.com/, many thanks to Rogier A. Kievit.

11.1 Magda Kouřilová, *Communicative characteristics of reviews of scientific papers written by non-native users of English* (published in Endocrine Regulations Vol. 32, 107 No. 114, 1998)— www.aepress.sk/endo/full/er0298g.pdf.; Sweitzer BJ, Cullen DJ, *How well does a journal's peer review process function? A survey of authors' opinions* (JAMA1994;272:152–3; Juan Miguel Campanario, *Have referees rejected some of the most-cited articles of all times?* Journal of the American Society for Information Science, Volume 47 Issue 4, April 1996.

Chapter 12

(1) https://www.uow.edu.au/~bmartin/pubs/08jspsrr.html; (2,3) Personal communications. Some subsections of this chapter drew ideas from the NOFOMA 2007 review guidelines.

Chapter 13

(1–3) Personal communications.

Index

This book is indexed by chapters and subsections.

Numbers in **bold** refer to complete chapters (e.g. **5** = Chapter 5), numbers not in bold refer to subsections (e.g. 5.7 = Section 7 in Chapter 5).

© Springer International Publishing Switzerland 2016
A. Wallwork, *English for Academic Correspondence*,
English for Academic Research, DOI 10.1007/978-3-319-26435-6

Printed in Great
Britain
by Amazon